Carmela's Table

Vittorio Rossi

CARMELA'S TABLE

A Carpenter's Trilogy

A Chronicle in Three Plays

Part Two

Talonbooks

Vancouver

Talonbooks
P.O. Box 2076, Vancouver, British Columbia, Canada V6B 3S3
www.talonbooks.com

Typeset in New Baskerville and printed and bound in Canada.

First Printing: 2008

The publisher gratefully acknowledges the financial support of the Canada
Council for the Arts; the Government of Canada through the Book
Publishing Industry Development Program; and the Province of British
Columbia through the British Columbia Arts Council and the Book
Publishing Tax Credit for our publishing activities.

Library and Archives Canada Cataloguing in Publication

Rossi, Vittorio, 1961–
    Carmela's table / Vittorio Rossi.

A play.
ISBN 978-0-88922-594-7

    1. Italian Canadians–Drama. 2. Italians–Canada–Drama.
I. Title.

PS8585.O8425C37 2008   C812'.54   C2008-903039-7

In loving memory of my mother

Carmela's Table was first produced by Centaur Theatre Company in Montréal, Quebec. Its premiere presentation took place on October 5, 2006 with the following cast:

SILVIO .... Richard Zeppieri
CARMELA .... Anita La Selva
FILOMENA .... Mary Long
DAVE .... Guido Cocomello
NEVA .... Nadia Verrucci

Director: Gordon McCall
Set design: John Dinning
Costume design: Susana Vera
Lighting design: Luc Prairie
Production manager: Howard Mendelsohn
General manager: Charles Childs
Stage manager: Robert Harding
Assistant stage manager: Rob Middleton

Characters

SILVIO ROSATO, *37, a carpenter, and a decorated World War II veteran.*

CARMELA ROSATO, *27, Silvio's wife, a seamstress.*

FILOMENA ROSATO, *61, Silvio's mother.*

DAVE DAMONTI, *28, a policeman.*

NEVA ESPOSITO, *40, an administrative secretary of the emergency ward at the Royal Victoria Hospital. Carmela's confidante and neighbour.*

Place

Ville Emard, Montréal.

Time

Spring, 1957.

ACT ONE

Scene One: Morning.

Scene Two: A few hours later.

Scene Three: Around midnight that day.

ACT TWO

Scene One: Morning of the following day.

Scene Two: Later that night.

Scene Three: The next morning.

If pa's eyes were windows into a world so deadly and true
You couldn't stop me from looking but you kept me from crawlin' through
And if it's a funny old world, mama, where a little boy's wishes come true
Well I got a few left in my pocket and a special one just for you.

Bruce Springsteen from "The Wish"

Act One

Scene One

Ville Emard, Montréal, 1957. The backyard of a small bungalow. A porch extends the width of the house. A baby carriage, and a rocking chair adorn the porch. The yard has a carpenter's work station, a few potted plants, and a patio with a bench and chairs. In the front of the yard lies a wooden canopy swing.

The interior is made up of a fully equipped kitchen at the centre of which are a table and chairs. An entrance leads to the rest of the house off-stage.

The bungalow sits between two duplexes. Windows on the upper levels look out into the backyard. Gates lead to either duplex and out to the front of the house off-stage.

On rise, a beautiful, vivacious young woman is sitting on the rocking chair breastfeeding a six-month-old baby boy. This is CARMELA ROSATO. She is twenty-seven years old and has virtually a perennial smile on her.

CARMELA

(singing)

Lo sai che i papaveri son alti alti alti

E tu sei piccolino, e tu sei piccolino

Lo sai che i papaveri son alti alti alti

(English translation)

You know that poppies grow tall tall tall

And you are very small small small

You know that poppies grow tall tall tall

| Sei nato paperino, che cosa ci voi far | *You were born a little duckling what can be done* |

She continues breastfeeding as she admires and comforts her child.

CARMELA

You're my little prince, aren't you? You're my little prince, aren't you. There you go, there you go! (*switches breast*) I will never let you go, no I won't. I'll always be there, yes I will. Yes I will.

DAVE DAMONTI enters the yard. He is a twenty-eight-year-old policeman. He is dressed in full uniform.

DAVE

Buon giorno, Carmela.

CARMELA

Buon giorno, Dave.

DAVE

Oh … uh … Where's Silvio? (*turns away shyly*)

CARMELA

Working. Where else is he going to be? Can you get me that blanket, please.

DAVE does his best to avoid looking at CARMELA's breasts, as he crosses to the swing to get the blanket.

DAVE

He didn't come back?

CARMELA

At this time? No.

DAVE

I need to talk to Silvio.

CARMELA

We paid your mother the rent.

DAVE
I know.

CARMELA
You want some coffee? (*rises to place the infant in the carriage*)
I don't know how to make that crazy coffee they drink
here, so I'll make you an espresso.

DAVE
That's fine.

CARMELA
What are you looking at?

DAVE
Oh … uh … a sparrow. Isn't that a nice bird.

CARMELA
That's all you see here are sparrows.

DAVE
Yes … well, how is the little boy?

CARMELA
He has an appetite this one. (*places the blanket on the baby*)
Isn't that right, my little prince. Look at him. (*buttons up her
blouse*)

DAVE
That's a handsome little boy you got there.

CARMELA
Come and see him. Come say hello to Luciano before he
falls asleep.

DAVE
Carmela, listen … (*crosses to the carriage*)

CARMELA
Do you want a panino? (*crosses into the kitchen*)

DAVE
No. I'm on duty.

CARMELA

You could still eat.

DAVE

It's fine. I had breakfast. Hey there, little boy. Aren't you a handsome little fellow. Yes you are. Yes you are. My God. They're so peaceful at this age.

CARMELA

(*re-enters with a wooden box potted with small tomato plants*) It's time for you and Georgette to have one.

DAVE

Oh, yes, well, she's pregnant.

CARMELA

She is? Oh my God. Auguro. Your mother will be so happy.

DAVE

She is, she is, I told her yesterday. Are those flowers?

CARMELA

Tomatoes. I brought the seeds myself from Italy. They've taken root, and now I can plant them in my garden.

DAVE

What garden?

CARMELA

There's all sorts of land by the railroad tracks. Look at this, do you know what that is? (*DAVE shakes his head.*) This is melanzana. How do you say … ?

DAVE

Oh, uh, eggplant.

CARMELA

And this?

DAVE

That looks like parsley.

CARMELA
That's parsley. This is basil. And this here ... my
favourite ... bietola ... how do you say that in English ...

DAVE
Uhh ... Swiss chard ... This is all from Italy?

CARMELA
Yes. The seeds all come from back home. So now we have a
little bit of Campobasso right here in Montréal. And inside
I have beans just ready to be planted.

DAVE
Listen, Carmela, you shouldn't be out here with your ...
exposed like that. You should do that inside. People here
are not used to seeing that.

CARMELA
How do I feed the baby? Back home everyone breastfed
their child.

DAVE
Here too, but this isn't the village. People here are more
discreet about these things. They're not used to seeing ...
you know ...

CARMELA
Breasts?

DAVE
Well, yes. I mean not in that capacity.

CARMELA
In what capacity are they used to seeing them?

DAVE
No, I mean, yes. People see ...

CARMELA
Breasts?

DAVE

Yes, but out in the open, that's another thing. Word goes around. You have a fifteen-year-old kid just across the lane, he could be peeking. I mean it isn't right.

CARMELA

It isn't right that a young boy sees a mother feed her child? My God, what kind of people live here?

DAVE

The French and the English, they comport themselves differently. (*pause*) Comport … uh … they expose themselves in a different … you know … manner.

CARMELA

What are they, savages?

DAVE

That's what they think of us. One of your neighbours is complaining.

CARMELA

For breastfeeding a child out in the open? Have I broken the law?

DAVE

No. God, no.

CARMELA

So, I haven't broken the law. One of my neighbours complained, and you come here to tell me that I did nothing wrong by law, but that I should not do it anymore.

DAVE

There you go. We understand each other.

CARMELA

What's the penalty if I keep feeding my child out in the backyard?

DAVE

There is no penalty. It's not the law. I'm just telling you to be more discreet.

CARMELA steps back into the kitchen.

DAVE

Don't worry, Carmela. You'll get used to it. People here aren't as open about these things as they are back in Italy.

CARMELA

Do they think everyone in Italy runs around naked?

DAVE

Well, no. I don't think ... I don't know what they think, actually. I just know that the new immigrants are different.

CARMELA

(*enters the yard with two cups of espresso*) You mean the Italians?

DAVE

I mean immigrants in general.

CARMELA

What immigrants? All I see here in *Ville Amore* are Italian families buying houses. So when they say immigrants, they mean Italians.

DAVE

Well, yes, I guess you can say that. (*sips his espresso*)

CARMELA

Dio mio. Com'è strana la gente. (*sips her espresso*)

DAVE

(*coughing*) It's not ... that ... they're strange ... (*coughing*) It's that ...

CARMELA

You want some water?

DAVE

No. I'm fine. This coffee is ... very tasty.

CARMELA

You want more?

DAVE

No. I'm fine. Carmela, I'm here on official business. I need to talk to Silvio.

A bell clanging is heard from off-stage.

NEVA

(*off-stage*) Carmela! Carmela! Ligurio is here!

NEVA ESPOSITO appears at the upper window next door. She is a charming forty-year-old woman with a calm disposition.

NEVA

Carmela! Subito! Get your knives and scissors!

CARMELA

What's all that ringing?

NEVA

It's Ligurio! He sharpens knives and scissors. Do you have anything to sharpen?

CARMELA

Yes I do, but I don't have any money right now!

NEVA

Don't worry about it! I'll take care of it! Dave, I heard Georgette is pregnant!

DAVE

Yes. It's six weeks!

NEVA

It's about time you did something in that bed! Go see if your mother needs any of her knives sharpened. (*exits*)

DAVE

It's okay, her knives are sharp!

CARMELA

Keep an eye on the baby. (*exits into the house*)

DAVE

He's fine! Look, I'll come back later ...

CARMELA
(*off-stage*) Wait, wait, I want to hear what you have to say!

DAVE
We can deal with this tonight. I got a patrol car out front, my captain is waiting for me at the station. And he doesn't like to be kept waiting, he likes to eat every half hour. I can't look after the baby right now.

NEVA enters the yard with some knives and some material for a dress.

NEVA
Where's my little prince? Let me see that little boy. Look at him. He's so adorable. Aren't you my little angel?

DAVE
Do you have to shout things out like that?

NEVA
Good morning, handsome. (*shouting off towards the front*) Ligurio! Aspetta! I'll be right there! Don't you have any knives to sharpen?

DAVE
No.

NEVA
What about your gun? So you can shoot straight.

DAVE
You don't sharpen a gun, Neva!

NEVA
You're so cute when you get angry.

CARMELA comes running out with a sizeable knife and scissors. She hands them to NEVA.

NEVA
Madonna, che cortello!

CARMELA

Silvio made it. With this, you hold a chicken down, you chop the head off. Once you kill a pig, fai na tagliata cosi, a cut right down the middle.

DAVE

Carmela, you can't bring farm animals into the yard!

NEVA

We're going to raise some rabbits, chickens, pigs, isn't that right, Carmela?

CARMELA

And sheep, make a nice arrosto d'agnello.

DAVE

This isn't a farm!

NEVA

We're joking, my God. What brings you here anyway?

CARMELA

I'm not allowed to use my breasts.

DAVE

I didn't say that.

NEVA

Is that neighbour complaining again? She can breastfeed her child out in the open. A woman has rights.

DAVE

That's fine. But do it in the house.

NEVA

Here's the material I promised.

CARMELA

(*examines it*) Oh, thank you, Neva. You're so kind.

NEVA

Will you stop that clanging! You're going to wake up the baby! I'm coming!

NEVA exits. Eventually the clanging stops.

DAVE
I'll come back later. Can you make sure Silvio calls me at the station when he comes in. It's very important.

CARMELA
Did something happen?

DAVE
I'd rather discuss this with Silvio.

NEVA enters the yard.

NEVA
He'll be done in a few minutes.

CARMELA
There's enough for two dresses here. How can I repay you?

NEVA
My friend gets it for free. It's left over. They'll throw it out anyway.

CARMELA
What a shame to throw it out. Voi un caffè?

NEVA
Yes, please.

CARMELA
Dave? More coffee? (*steps into the kitchen*)

DAVE
No. No. Not for me. (*to NEVA*) You should not be encouraging Carmela to breastfeed out in the open like that.

NEVA
Ma-please. Go arrest someone.

DAVE
People are complaining. It gives us Italians a bad name.

NEVA

Let them complain. That's all they do, is complain
complain complain. This neighbourhood needs a little life.

CARMELA

(*enters with more coffee*) I know just the perfect dress to
make.

NEVA

Shouldn't you be working?

CARMELA

He's here to arrest Silvio.

DAVE

I didn't say that.

NEVA

Because of the shouting?

DAVE

There was shouting? When?

NEVA

Yesterday. Madonna che casino. Me and Mike came over to
see what all the fuss was about.

DAVE

We've been getting complaints from other neighbours too.
What happened?

CARMELA

It was between Silvio and his mother ... going on about his
trip to Chicago last year. Silvio and his mother are always at
each other. The littlest thing sets them off. He tries his best
to avoid an argument. But that Filomena, she's a stubborn
mule when she doesn't get her way. And me, I'm caught in
the middle.

DAVE

You have to tell me if he laid a hand on you. People don't
put up with that here.

CARMELA
And in Italy they do?

DAVE
You know what I mean.

CARMELA
No, I don't know. What do you think Italy is, a country of barefooted people, women running around with their breasts exposed walking with sticks and eating from trees? Family problems were taken care of inside the home. There was no need for the police.

NEVA
You tell him, Carmela.

DAVE
I understand that. But when a neighbour is afraid for his safety, then it becomes a police matter.

CARMELA
This neighbour is afraid of us? Who is it?

DAVE
I can't tell you that.

NEVA
I know who it is.

CARMELA
I wish we never came here.

DAVE
You have to learn to control Silvio. He has a temper. I've seen it playing cards. Now tell me what happened.

CARMELA
It's all Filomena: "Why did you go to Chicago? Why this, why that?" And that set him off.

DAVE
Why did he go?

CARMELA
He went for a little help. Silvio will do anything for me and
the children. This is his family, this is all he has.

NEVA
It was a simple argument between a mother and her son.

DAVE
Oh, no.

NEVA
What's wrong?

DAVE
The coffee. It gives me the runs. Excuse me. (*He runs
inside.*)

CARMELA
It's all those dreams Silvio's been having. The war. England.
When he was a prisoner. In Belgium when we were alone,
just me him and the girls, he would go straight to sleep.
And now with his mother. One nightmare after another.

NEVA
Did something happen between them?

CARMELA
Parliamo doppo a quattr'occhi.

NEVA
What did you say? We'll talk later with four eyes?

CARMELA
Yes.

NEVA
What an interesting phrase.

CARMELA
Yes. Two people, four eyes. That's what you say when you
want to talk alone with that person.

NEVA
I learn something new everyday with you, Carmela.

CARMELA

Ah, let it go. No one can solve this. Do people really think we're savages?

NEVA

Oh, let them talk. They'll get used to it.

CARMELA

We're just trying to live. We don't bother anyone.

NEVA

Forget about Dave. He's a good boy. He's just doing his job. Besides, what are they going to do? They can't stop the Italians from immigrating. Believe me. My family has been here since the twenties. You think it's tough now. When my father came here there were hardly any Italians. Ville Emard was nothing but farms, factories and foundries. It was harder then. You have it better now. Look how they're building up Monk Boulevard.

CARMELA

Ohhh, Neva, I love *Boolewarde Monk*, that street has everything I need.

DAVE

(*entering*) There's a hole in the wall!

CARMELA

Eh m'beh?

DAVE

How did it get there? Was that Silvio? How did he do that?

CARMELA

Once the argument got going. *Boom-a-da*!

DAVE

Carmela. You don't go punching holes in other people's houses. If my mother sees that, she'll raise the rent.

CARMELA

He'll fix it.

DAVE

Is Silvio hurt?

CARMELA

Hurt? For punching a hole in the wall? You're funny. It'll
take more than a punch to hurt Silvio. (*She clears the coffee
cups, and exits.*)

DAVE

My God, Neva, what the hell is going on here?

NEVA

It'll take some time for them to get adjusted. Carmela has
only been here two months. Give them all some time.

DAVE

People are complaining.

NEVA

Tell them to mind their own business.

DAVE

He punched a hole in the wall.

CARMELA enters with coffee.

CARMELA

How are your parents?

NEVA

I took them for their medical. They're fine. They'll live to
be a hundred and nine.

DAVE

Ladies, please. May I finish my questions here?

NEVA

Oh, Carmela, isn't this fun. We're being interrogated.

DAVE

This isn't an interrogation—Look, you should show more
respect for a man in uniform.

CARMELA

I can make a nicer uniform than that. Me, I'd put a nice blue stripe on the side here. It would add a little style, and it keeps the line and the look of authority.

DAVE

This isn't funny.

CARMELA

I know. You should let me talk to your captain. I can make new uniforms for everyone.

DAVE

The entire Montreal Police Force?

CARMELA

Is that a lot of people?

DAVE

Yes it's a lot—Look … there's a hole in the wall, and you two are out here making fun of me.

NEVA

I'm sorry, Dave. But this investigation here is a little ridiculous.

DAVE

They were going to send a couple of French cops. I'm doing you a favour here.

CARMELA

French policemen? Why?

DAVE

Carmela, look, that's why I'm here. I didn't want you to get involved, but Silvio …

CARMELA

Silvio is my husband, I am involved.

DAVE

Silvio threatened the contractor on the job site. (*checks his notebook*) A Mr. Martin. He threatened him, and walked off

29

the job. Now I need to find him. Understand? Martin called the police station. I said I would talk to Silvio. I'm doing this as a courtesy.

The ringing out front starts up again.

CARMELA

E finiscila, mannaggia la miseria! (*exits by the gate*)

NEVA

Carmela, wait! You don't have to upset her like that.

DAVE

Neva, I'm already in over my head on this one. We received a complaint, and it has to be dealt with. You don't go around threatening people. He's not even a citizen yet.

NEVA

I'm sure it was nothing. Silvio wouldn't do that. Watch the baby. (*exits*)

DAVE

I'm on duty, I gotta go! (*looks over to the baby*) What's wrong there, little boy? Shouldn't you be sleeping? Uh? (*picks up the baby*) There you go. Nothing to be afraid of. You know my wife's gonna have a boy. I just know it. Then you and my son will play together ... oh man ... you don't smell too good. Uh ... let me see ... (*He places the baby back in the carriage. He crosses to the gate and calls out.*) Carmela!

SILVIO ROSATO enters the kitchen. He is thirty-seven years old. He has a handsome, determined, powerful look about him. He is dressed in work clothes and carries his toolbox. He feels the top of the kitchen table and shakes his head. He enters the yard.

DAVE

Buon giorno. Look, we have to talk about what happened at work today.

SILVIO checks the carriage. He goes to his toolbox and takes out a small wooden hammer, a toy. He lays it gently into the baby's carriage. He leans in and kisses the child.

SILVIO

You know, Dave, you can begin to tell the character of a man by the way he greets you. Buon giorno. That's very general. Buon giorno, Dave. Now I've made it personal. A personal greeting to you. It's a sign of respect. If I offer my hand, then you can tell by the squeeze and the shake if you really care. Now. Show me you care.

DAVE

Buon giorno, Silvio. (*shakes his hand*)

SILVIO

Isn't he something? Look at his hands. These are the hands of a builder. Isn't that right, little boy. Everything I do, I do for you. You know that? Ah? No one is going to push you around. (*crosses to his work station and puts down his toolbox*)

> *CARMELA and NEVA enter with the knives and they're laughing hysterically.*

NEVA

Did you see that, I can't believe it. Oh my God ...

CARMELA

O Dio ... mi fa crepare di risate ... Silvio ...

NEVA

Oh my God ... Ligurio ... he ... as I went to pay him ... he farted ... he excused himself ...

CARMELA

... And then he farted again ... madonna che puzza ...

NEVA

He had this look on his face ... he kept apologizing ...

CARMELA

But he kept farting ... I asked him if he needed to use the bathroom.

NEVA

And he says ... he says ... no ... I would rather just fart my way through this one.

CARMELA

O Dio … che cafone … (*takes the baby and exits into the house*)

SILVIO

How is the dottoressa?

NEVA

Buon giorno, Silvio. And stop calling me doctor, I'm no doctor.

SILVIO

You work for doctors in a hospital. Back home that's as good as a doctor.

NEVA

I work in the emergency ward, I'm just an administrative secretary. Believe me, the Royal Victoria Hospital does not consider me medical staff. But I'll accept your compliment.

DAVE

Silvio, what did you do on the job today? We got a call, a complaint from your boss. That you threatened him.

SILVIO

He said I threatened him? (*enters into the kitchen and gets a glass of wine*)

DAVE

(*looks at his notebook as he follows SILVIO inside*) Yes. Mr. Martin. You threatened his life. What happened? Look, Silvio, you don't go around threatening people like that. He's the boss. He could make it real difficult for you. These English guys have connections, especially those with money.

SILVIO

First of all he's not English. A real Englishman has more manners than that. Martin is not his real name. His name is Martino. An Italian born here who changed his name to sound Canadian.

DAVE

What did you do to him? Silvio, they were going to send
two French cops. I came as a courtesy. Now tell me.

SILVIO

Dave. He threatened me. And my family.

DAVE

What do you mean?

SILVIO

I refused to work the compromises he asked for on the job.
I packed my tools and told him to find another carpenter.
He said if I don't finish the job today, he was going to
report me to the Immigration Authorities. (*crosses back into
the yard*)

DAVE

(*follows him out*) Report you on what?

SILVIO

He was going to make something up. Now, if I'm deported,
my family here has no future. That's a threat to my family.
And for what? Because I won't compromise my work. I said
to him, very calmly, "You go anywhere near the
Immigration Office, I will kill you twice."

NEVA

Twice?

SILVIO

That's right, Neva. Twice.

DAVE

How can you kill a man two times?

SILVIO

Oh, believe me. It's possible. First you destroy everything
that's inside him. His very essence. You make him see and
believe what a sorry pathetic excuse of a human being he
is. When he comes to realize that his life is worthless, he's

already dead. He will then beg you to destroy him. That's how you kill a man two times.

NEVA

That's still a threat.

SILVIO

I was defending my family.

CARMELA enters the backyard with the baby.

DAVE

Why don't we go to the station and sort this thing out.

SILVIO

If this country doesn't wake up, it will die. I can't work when I'm told by the builder to compromise the job. I'm a carpenter, I build things to last, not to fall apart.

NEVA .

Silvio, you can't just walk out on a job. People won't hire you.

SILVIO

You think I can't find work? I told Martino, you want to build houses, you have to build them so they last. He's building houses all over Ville La Salle. Ever take a look across the train tracks, Dave? It's all swamp land. He's building houses on unstable ground. When my little boy is a young man, those houses will be sinking. Understand? What he's doing is criminal.

DAVE

He must be following the building codes.

SILVIO

What building codes? No one follows any building codes. People like Martino are laughing at the authorities here. No one says anything. When you build a floor, you're supposed to use two-by-eight floor joists spaced every sixteen inches. He wants to use two-by-six floor joists every twenty to twenty-four inches. When they start building the second floor, with the scaffolding, equipment, and the men, the floor will collapse under the weight. I could already picture the damage. And I don't want to be there when it all comes crashing down.

CARMELA

(*places the baby in the carriage*) Did you try reasoning with him?

SILVIO

You can't reason with a greedy man. He wants to save money on construction material, he just sees the profit, not the house. I see the house first.

CARMELA

We have no money coming in.

SILVIO

Carmela, please.

CARMELA

(*picks up the little wooden hammer from the carriage*) What's this?

SILVIO

I made it for the little boy. A wooden hammer. As soon as he starts walking he can start banging things around just like his father.

CARMELA

You must be hungry. I'll heat up those beans.

SILVIO

I found the land for the garden. We can start planting.

CARMELA

You did? Oh my God, I can't wait to get started. (*enters into the kitchen*)

NEVA

You two are so efficient, it's amazing. You build, you plant.

SILVIO

During the war, you had to learn how to do everything.
The more you knew, the better your chances of surviving.
Here everyone has things done for them. I don't see any
skill. How much did you just spend sharpening those
knives?

NEVA

Ten cents.

SILVIO

With ten cents, I could've bought some food for the baby.

NEVA

We just don't think of these things here.

SILVIO

What's his name, the sharpener ... Ligurio ... he's relying
on your ignorance so he can make a living.

*FILOMENA ROSATO enters. She is a sixty-one-year-old woman.
Her looks belie her age. She is the epitome of strength and
survival. She has an air of grace and pride about her. Above
all, like her son, she shows no fear. She carries bags full of
chicory plant, and a few envelopes.*

FILOMENA

Sta sera si mangia. Cicoria per tutti. You should learn to
start eating this.

DAVE

How can you eat that?

FILOMENA

Non ti la mangia la cicoria?

NEVA

You don't like chicory plant?

DAVE

That's like wild grass.

FILOMENA

I got it in the fields near the park. There's enough there to feed an army. You make a salad, see how good it is. (*to SILVIO*) What are you doing home so early? Shouldn't you be working? Why aren't you working?

DAVE

Silvio, please, let's go to the station to settle this. I have the car out front.

FILOMENA

What did you do?

SILVIO

Nothing. I'm going to plant a garden today. (*grabs a few plants and exits*)

FILOMENA

O Dio, don't start with me today. (*enters into the kitchen*) The mailman just came.

CARMELA

What's wrong with you now?

FILOMENA

I have to walk three kilometres to bring those two girls to school. The French school is two blocks away. Why would they refuse Maria and Liliana into the French school?

NEVA

It's better that they go to the English school.

SILVIO re-enters to get more plants.

FILOMENA

Those girls speak French, they learnt it in Belgium. It just breaks my heart that my two little angels have to walk all that distance. When we went to register them in the French school they refused us and pointed the way to the English school. You think that's nice?

SILVIO

I told them. My girls speak French. They don't know English.

FILOMENA

All immigrants ... which means the Italians, must go to English school. It's wrong.

SILVIO

She's right about that.

FILOMENA

At least I'm right about something.

SILVIO

This will come to hurt the French, you know. Not now, not even tomorrow. But in the future, they will have a big problem. They don't see it, but they are playing right into the hands of the English.

DAVE

What do you mean?

SILVIO

Dave, wake up. If every Italian, Spanish, Portuguese, Greek is refused entry into their schools, and they all start adapting to the English language, the English ways, the French will be outnumbered one day. They will be a minority in their own land. You can't stop us. We'll be calling over our sisters, cousins, nieces and nephews. It won't stop. The French should be making friends with us. Believe me, they don't want us as enemies. (*exits with more plants*)

DAVE

Will you at least come with me to the work site, so we can talk to Martino?

FILOMENA

What did he do?

CARMELA

He threatened the boss.

FILOMENA

Bella roba. We're not even settled here yet, and he's threatening the people who hire him.

SILVIO re-enters and crosses into the kitchen.

DAVE

Silvio, please ... this won't take long. I have to report to my captain, I have to tell him something. You think about it very carefully. You don't want a police report on you. And I can't stop my captain from sending over two other cops. And then there's that neighbour to deal with. He's always complaining. Silvio, I'm warning you. All I'm asking for is a simple apology.

SILVIO

(*erupting*) I did nothing wrong! I defended my family. And now I have to deal with a complaining neighbour who has a problem with Italians.

DAVE

The immigrants have to learn to mix with them, not the other way around.

SILVIO

Immigrants ... immigrants. Why don't you tell it like it is? What immigrants? These people need their houses built, who do they call? An Italian? You need a bricklayer, he's Italian! An electrician? He's Italian! You need to teach these people to cook and eat, who are they going to call? An Italian! Look around you, Dave. Ville Emard. This whole neighbourhood ... it's Italians that keep it alive, so don't you use their word ... immigrant ... on me. You could at least show me the courtesy and speak to me directly as an Italian. They want war! They don't know what war is. They surround themselves with their stupid laws and regulations to protect themselves ... their culture from being eaten alive by a people that just want to live their lives. They feel threatened, that's not my problem.

FILOMENA

Don't take it out on Dave.

SILVIO

Ever hear of ... "When in Rome, do as the Romans do?"

DAVE

Yes.

SILVIO

Well. There it is.

DAVE

You're not in Rome.

SILVIO

You sure about that? If all the labourers in the industries ... all the Italians who work the assembly lines, all the Italians who build the houses, lay the bricks, mend the clothes, cook the food, if all of them just stopped working, this whole city would be paralysed. As far as I'm concerned this is just another province of Rome. And they have the face to refuse my children into their schools.

DAVE

Look, Silvio, I'm not here to talk about the politics of the French.

SILVIO

Then don't. And another thing, next time you think you're doing my family a favour here, don't come with your gun. My little girls could come running in here. They don't need to see that. You could show me that courtesy.

DAVE

It's part of the uniform.

SILVIO

Ever fire a gun?

DAVE
Not in the line of duty.

SILVIO
Pray you never have to use it.

CARMELA
Dave, sit down and have some food with Silvio.

FILOMENA
Put more salt in those beans.

CARMELA
I know how to cook, Ma.

FILOMENA
The beans are a little scémo di sale.

CARMELA
Fine, I'll put more salt. Dave, please.

DAVE
It's okay, Carmela. He's right. I should've come here as a
friend, not as a policeman. I'll go on the work site, I'll talk
to Martino. I'll try to convince him not to press charges.
Thanks for the coffee, Carmela. Buona giornata a tutti.
Buon giorno, Silvio.

SILVIO
(*shakes his hand*) Buon lavoro, Dave. Dave. We'll get the
men together on Saturday, we'll play some Gin Rummy.

DAVE smiles and exits.

CARMELA
Here, Ma, this is a letter for you. From Italy.

FILOMENA
For me? Who would write to me? O che bello, Francesco
wrote. (*opens up the envelope and begins to read the letter*)

NEVA
Who's Francesco?

FILOMENA

He's one of my oldest friends. In my life, Francesco did the
most to help me and my Silvio. Oh, how I miss him. He says
here ... (*reading the letter*) "My dear Filomena, we miss you
so very much. How sad it was the day you left with Carmela
and those beautiful children. My hope is that you find.
peace and happiness in your new home with your son."
(*holding back tears*) I'll never forget that day. They came
from all over the valley to say good-bye to me. Ah ...
anyway ... it says here ... Oh, look at this, Stella had her
baby. Madonna, she's a rabbit that one. Okay. (*reads*) "I'm
sorry to inform you that Filippo is dead. His death was fast
and we are all sad that he is no longer with us." Oh,
poverino ... I will miss Filippo.

NEVA

My condolences, I'm sorry for your loss, was he close to the
family?

FILOMENA

We had Filippo for over ten years. The way he climbed
those hills.

NEVA

What do you mean you *had* him for ten years?

FILOMENA

Filippo is a donkey. You know ... a chooch.

CARMELA

Keep reading, Ma.

FILOMENA

(*reads*) "Filomena, you've lived a hard life and a virtuous
one. You deserve all the good that God can give you."
Oh ... that Francesco ... what a nice man ... (*reads*) "Think
well of us, as we have good memories of you and your son.
And you tell your son, you tell that dear Silvio how proud
we are of him for what he did in Chicago. How courageous
he was to go face his father in Chicago."

SILVIO

Ma, please …

FILOMENA

This is from Francesco … right from his mouth … (*reads*)
"What your Silvio endured is something no one should
have to go through. Here's a man who fought a war in
Egypt. In the desert. Almost got killed. Was wounded.
Captured by the British. Four years as a prisoner of war in
England. Survived it all. A courageous and noble man. May
he find the peace he deserves in his life. You know,
Filomena, your son wanted so many answers when he came
back from the war." Ah, who can forget the day you
arrived … Silvio, tell Neva what a day that was …

SILVIO

Ma …

FILOMENA

Okay. I'll tell you another time. (*reads*) "The day after he
came back from the war, your Silvio walked the entire
valley, to all thirteen villages, to speak to his closest friends.
He asked them if … " (*She suddenly is silent, and reads to
herself.*) Dio mio! O Dio!

CARMELA

Did someone die?

FILOMENA

Worse. (*hands the letter to CARMELA, and then walks right up to
SILVIO*) You had the face, after all I went through, to
question my motives. (*pause*) Where did you find the
courage to even have such thoughts? About me! About
your mother! Come ti permetti! O Dio! I can't face this
anymore. After all I did for you. This is the way you repay
me. You never once in your life apologized for anything.
But for this, figlio mio, you will get down on your knees
and apologize. To me. Io sono tua madre. Pray that God
can show you the way, son, because I can't. (*The baby starts
to cry. She picks up the baby.*) Vieni con nonna. Carino mio.

43

(*to SILVIO*) You just don't know how to stop hurting people, do you? (*exits into the house with the baby*)

CARMELA

Silvio, why don't you go back to work. (*SILVIO snatches the letter from CARMELA and reads it.*) Go back to work.

SILVIO

I'm not going anywhere. I'm going to build a table for the kitchen.

CARMELA

But we have one.

SILVIO

You call that a table? We need a new table, and I'm going to build it. (*hands the letter back to CARMELA and exits into the house*)

CARMELA

My, God, this is never going to end.

NEVA

What happened?

CARMELA

(*peruses the letter*) Dio mio ... with a wounded leg he decides ... Silvio decides ... after the war ... to walk another thirty miles ...

NEVA

Why would he do that?

CARMELA

He must have been curious.

NEVA

About what?

CARMELA

His mother. You know he had no father. Eduardo that *vigliacco* abandoned my Silvio when he was a little baby. No bigger than what Luciano is now. I can't imagine leaving

him for anything. That's what Silvio's father did. He left a
child to die. And one day I will give him my own mouth
full. But that's for later.

NEVA

You said Silvio was curious.

CARMELA

He wanted to know if maybe his mother had anything to do
with Eduardo never coming back for her and the children.
So he walked thirty miles of hills going from village to
village investigating his mother. He asked those very close
to him if ... if Filomena ... was playing, you know ... the
male femena ...

NEVA

A whore.

CARMELA

Not quite a whore, but a loose woman.

NEVA

Was she?

CARMELA

No. That woman was a saint. That's what he found out.

NEVA

But Silvio's father married another woman. She was free to
move on.

CARMELA

There's no divorce. In the eyes of the Church, she is still a
married woman. It's her husband that's the sinner. Silvio
discovered that his mother was a righteous woman. This
letter praises Silvio for being the good son. That he had the
courage to question his mother's fidelity.

NEVA

Courage? What was he thinking? Her honour was
questioned. I don't know how Silvio is going to fix this.

CARMELA

What's done is done. Filomena is insulted, and now the war begins.

SILVIO enters the yard.

SILVIO

Carmela, where's my suit?

CARMELA

It's in the room. What are you going to do with the suit?

SILVIO

I need it for my immigration picture. I'll go tomorrow.

CARMELA

I'll prepare it for you. Come inside and eat. (*exits*)

NEVA

Silvio, this letter ...

SILVIO

That's not on my mind right now. I'll take care of my mother later. (*pause*) Neva, listen. Yesterday ... during the argument ... and I swear to you ... the words I exchanged were with my mother, not Carmela. At one point Carmela had enough, and she ... raised her voice ... you know ... and she ... how do you say ... she was struggling for breath.

NEVA

She was hyperventilating?

SILVIO

Yes. That's it.

NEVA

Have you seen that before?

SILVIO

No.

NEVA

Does she have asthma? Was she having an asthmatic attack?

SILVIO

No. She doesn't have asthma. You have to look into this for me. You work at the hospital, I don't know where to go.

NEVA

What is it?

SILVIO

Two days before we get married, Carmela fell ill with a very bad fever. We all thought we were going to lose her. She pulled through, thank God, but I never liked the look of it. They called it rheumatic fever. What do you know about that?

NEVA

Rheumatic fever?

SILVIO

It isn't dangerous, is it?

NEVA

Look. You can survive the fever. But it leaves scar tissue in the heart valves. It creates an irregular heartbeat.

SILVIO

An irregular heartbeat?

NEVA

Yes. It's time Carmela went to see a doctor. Why didn't she tell me this?

SILVIO

She's always concerned about other people, she puts herself last all the time.

NEVA

Well you're going to have to step up, and learn to calm down. Understand? You think it's easy being a mother?

SILVIO

Things set me off.

NEVA
Why?

SILVIO
I don't know. I wish I knew.

NEVA
This thing with your mother. What were you thinking?
After all that your mother did for you, you question her
honour?

SILVIO
That was twelve years ago.

NEVA
It doesn't matter. You have to fix this. Now you listen to me,
you *coccialone* you. Carmela does more for others than for
herself. It's up to you to give her something back.
Understand? Take care of the family. Your kids need you.
Carmela needs you.

CARMELA
(*entering*) Lunch is ready. You want me to bring it out here?

NEVA
Not for me, Carmela, I have to go. Me and Mike will be by
later tonight. (*She kisses CARMELA.*) You're such an angel.
Ciao, Silvio. (*exits*)

CARMELA
Come on. Don't let it get cold.

SILVIO
Carmela. Come over here.

CARMELA
I have things to do.

SILVIO
Will you come over here.

CARMELA
This thing with your mother.

SILVIO
Don't worry about my mother, I'll take care of her. (*moves to kiss her*)

CARMELA
Will you stop.

SILVIO
Come on. Why so serious?

CARMELA
We have no money coming in.

SILVIO
Don't worry about it.

CARMELA
The neighbour could be watching. Come in and eat.

SILVIO
Carmela ... Carmela ... wait. Look behind me. Over my right shoulder, to your left. Do you see the curtain moving?

CARMELA
No.

SILVIO
Okay. Keep looking. (*turns around suddenly*) There, did you see it?

CARMELA
Yes. I saw the curtain move.

SILVIO
That's him. That's the neighbour that's complaining about us.

CARMELA
He seemed like such a nice man.

SILVIO
Caress the back of my hair.

CARMELA
What?

SILVIO
Just do it. Good. Now, put your hand in my pocket.

CARMELA
Silvio!

SILVIO
Will you just do it.

CARMELA
What if your mother sees?

SILVIO
Don't worry about her. (*CARMELA has her hand in his pocket.*) Good. Now kiss me. Okay. Kiss me again, but try to see if those curtains are moving.

CARMELA
I can't kiss you and see the curtains at the same time.

SILVIO
Here let me try. (*He spins her around and plants a deep wet kiss on her.*) Yeah, he's watching. (*He leads CARMELA to the swing. She takes a seat.*) He's going to learn what love is all about.

CARMELA
You really think he's watching?

SILVIO
See for yourself.

CARMELA
Those curtains are shaking now.

SILVIO
That *pezzo di merde*. He wants to watch Italians make love. Talk as if you're saying you love me.

CARMELA
I love you ...

SILVIO
Well say it like you mean it …

CARMELA
I love you …

SILVIO
Okay. That's not bad. I have an even better idea … (*runs inside*)

CARMELA
Madonna, che dramma!

SILVIO has opened the window, and has propped up a phonograph so that the sound is directed outside.

CARMELA
Ma-che fai?

SILVIO
(*entering*) Ce lo faccio vedere io! Let him report this to the police.

Verdi's "Libiamo ne'lieti calici" from La Traviata is blasting on the phonograph.

CARMELA
Silvio …

SILVIO
Sshhh … sshhh … (*singing*) "Libiamo, libiamo ne'lieti calici che la bellezza infiora."

CARMELA
Silvio …

SILVIO
Carmela …

They kiss. Soon, the passion overwhelms them, and so they are not pretending anymore. The kissing is passionate. Soon, he is on top of her. They continue to kiss as the music plays, and the lights fade slowly to black.

Scene Two

A few hours later. CARMELA is sewing the hem on her dress. FILOMENA is separating the tender chicory leaves from the harder ones.

FILOMENA

I will not have my character questioned like that. Not by my son, my daughter. No one. I want my respect. I won't have it any other way. I worked too hard, sacrificed too much to give him a life, the least I could get in return is respect.

CARMELA

Don't take it that way, Ma. He was curious.

FILOMENA

Curious? To question his mother's integrity like that?

CARMELA

Oooofa! You know, I know, we all know what you did to keep your family together. Nobody doubts your integrity.

FILOMENA

Except my son. I hope you're sewing a blind stitch there.

CARMELA

Yes. Just like you taught me.

FILOMENA

My son was a good boy before he left for war. He developed a temper.

SILVIO enters carrying some wood, and examines it at his work station.

FILOMENA

Madonna, you actually entertained those thoughts. That I was playing the village whore ... that for some reason, I'm to blame for my husband never coming back for me and my children.

SILVIO quietly enters the kitchen and gets a glass and bottle of wine, and crosses back to his work station. Pours himself a drink and begins to work.

FILOMENA

My brother Peter ... when he went to Chicago ... he went for all of us. To open the way for us to get to America. He died. And Angelina that whore mistress ... and may God have mercy on her ... she took my husband away from me. And I stayed, Carmela, I stayed to raise my children. They had no father. They needed a mother. And I was there, Carmela. I was there. My whole life was sacrificed for my children. Nobody back home questioned my actions. Nobody. Except for my son. (*to SILVIO*) When I think of the questions you asked my friends. Was my mother with other men? Did she sleep around? Was she a whore? Did she give my father any reason to leave her? I just can't imagine even thinking such thoughts about a mother. And what must've been going through their minds to have such questions asked of them. To possibly place some doubt as to my actions.

SILVIO

Read the letter. (*exits by the side of the house*)

CARMELA

Nobody took Silvio's suspicions seriously, Ma. Did you ever think that when he asked those questions, that he was hoping, praying for the answers he got? He wanted to hear those good things about you. He wanted to have his suspicions buried for good. He needed to know once and for all who he could trust in his life. And it all begins with you.

FILOMENA

I don't think he'll ever be satisfied.

CARMELA

Why would he have brought you here with us? Why did he make you part of our family? He married me, and his place

is with me and the children. But he took you in with us
because it's his turn to take care of you now. Can't you look
at the positive side of his actions? Everywhere he went they
told him you were a saint.

FILOMENA
I'm not a saint.

CARMELA
You are a saint. You're a saintly woman.

FILOMENA
Don't call me that.

CARMELA
Okay, you're not a saint.

FILOMENA
See? You have doubts too.

CARMELA
You're driving me crazy. You'll both drive me to my grave
before I'm thirty.

FILOMENA
Why would you say such a thing?

CARMELA
You think it's easy being his wife, and your daughter-in-law?
Living all under the same roof, raising three children? *Dio
padre eterno!*

SILVIO
(*enters carrying more wood*) I don't want to hear this
anymore. If she actually read the whole letter, she would
learn of the relief in my soul when I heard she did the right
thing. But no, she can only see the negative side. And now I
have to pay for being curious.

FILOMENA
Why couldn't you trust me?

SILVIO

Read the letter! Why do you ignore the good things they say about me? Why? Why do you just want to fight?

FILOMENA

I curse the day I came to this godforsaken land!

SILVIO

Now we're getting somewhere.

FILOMENA

Look at you. You're turning into your father. You're as hateful as he is.

SILVIO

I'm just trying to build a table here. But you want to fight. Read the letter!

FILOMENA

I read what I had to read.

SILVIO

You spiteful, hateful—You drop this, or I will put you on the first boat back to Italy. (*finishes his drink and exits into the house*)

FILOMENA

You will live to regret these words. I want an apology!

CARMELA

For the sake of the kids, can't you just bury the past. Please. He made a mistake. Forgive him. Forgive him and move on. We all have to. For the children.

SILVIO

(*re-enters buttoning up his shirt*) I won't regret anything, Ma. You hear me? Not a thing! I had the right to be curious! I had the right to care about where I came from!

CARMELA

Where you going?

SILVIO

    I don't want to fight, Carmela. I just don't want to fight.

    NEVA appears at the upper window next door.

NEVA

    I can hear you all from my kitchen! My God, just let this thing go. (*exits*)

SILVIO

    She can't do it, Neva. She just can't.

FILOMENA

    Look at the way he talks to me. I am your mother. You will respect that.

SILVIO

    How can I respect you when all you do is question all my good motives.

FILOMENA

    Good motives? You call me a whore and that's supposed to be a good motive? And you call it curiosity? It's more than curiosity he's after. He wants answers to life that just aren't possible.

SILVIO

    That's right, Ma. I want answers. I want answers as to why I've been placed in hell here. I want to know why I can't find any peace within my own family. I want to know why you have this hatred for me.

    NEVA enters the backyard.

FILOMENA

    When did I ever hate you? When did I ever say that?

SILVIO

    Look at you. Look at how you continue to fight about something I did more than twelve years ago! What about what you did to me twelve years ago! I let it go. I don't keep bringing it up.

FILOMENA

(*pause*) I did nothing wrong. Nothing out of the ordinary.

SILVIO

That's right, so let it go. I just asked questions.

FILOMENA

You asked questions because you never trusted me. Never. I raised you and a daughter, with no husband, and what do I get in return? A hateful, distrustful son.

SILVIO

Is that what you think I am?

NEVA

Silvio, please, for the sake of the children ...

SILVIO

Don't throw my children in my face, Neva. Don't do that.

NEVA

Let's go somewhere and talk. Come on. Come with me. We'll talk, you can let it out.

SILVIO

Answer my question, Ma. You think I'm a hateful distrustful son?

FILOMENA

I said what I had to say.

SILVIO

Read the letter! Read the last paragraph. You choose to ignore the good that's there. Disgraziata!

NEVA

Silvio, please, don't talk to your mother like that.

CARMELA

Let them finish this, or it will never end.

SILVIO

Oh, it will end, Carmela. Trust me. It's going to end. You read the letter for yourself, Neva. They all heard back in

Italy what I did. They all heard back home, that I kept my honour when I visited my father in Chicago. When your husband called you a whore, I let him have it, Ma. I let him have what was coming to him. I defended your honour. And why, Ma? Why would I do that? Because I knew he was wrong. I knew you were the good mother. I believed what everyone said about you. Your reputation is untarnished. Your story … back home … will be set in stone … children will be told of your story … how a good woman once lived here … how a good mother … a godfearing woman … was abandoned for no good reason other than the infidelity of her husband. Nothing more. And that you survived it all. How … alone … she raised her children in spite of her husband's absence. But none of that counts. None of it.

FILOMENA
How can you have asked those questions about me?

SILVIO
That's right, Ma. I asked the right questions. Was my mother a whore? Was my mother a loose bitch with men? Did she parade them into the house like the village prostitute? Did she have more than one man at a time?

NEVA
Silvio …

SILVIO
Why did she never re-marry? Why did she stay alone? Was it for love of family? Or because she just liked to be with men?

FILOMENA
Shame on you, son, for even thinking such thoughts. I curse the day I had you.

SILVIO
I curse you, Ma. I curse the day you gave birth to me. I curse the day I survived in the desert. I should've died out there. I should've died, and then maybe you could think good thoughts of me. Because you can't, can you.

Somehow, you feel you let your life pass you by. You were twenty-four years old when your husband left you. And you've been alone since. And now you take it all out on me. Because I asked a few questions. When I come back, you will have put this to rest. You understand me? (*exits*)

FILOMENA
Lord help me. Watch over my son. Forgive him his actions.

CARMELA
See? Why would you say what you just said?

FILOMENA
Because he's still my son.

CARMELA
Why don't you tell him? To his face … tell him that you love him.

FILOMENA
Not after what he did.

CARMELA
He's right, you know. You have something inside you that despises him.

FILOMENA
Everything was fine before the war. It's what came after that I'm paying for.

The baby is heard crying. CARMELA exits into the house.

NEVA
Filomena your pride has been hurt.

FILOMENA
It's more than pride, Neva. It's my life he hurt. He disgraced everything I've done by asking those questions. I looked after him with everything I had. But to be spoken of like that. To be spoken to like this. That's a sin.

NEVA

I can't imagine what he was thinking. But please
understand, Silvio is still fighting a war. I've seen wounded
soldiers at the hospital, soldiers with mental wounds, they
develop a distrust of people. They question everything
that's around them. There's a lot that he does that he just
can't control yet.

CARMELA

(*off-stage*) I'm going to feed the baby.

NEVA

Come out here.

CARMELA

(*off-stage*) I don't want to start that again.

NEVA

Oh, forget about that damned neighbour! You come out
here and feed the baby!

CARMELA

(*enters with the baby*) There you go … Zia Neva is here to see
you.

NEVA

Let me see this little angel … oh … look at him …

FILOMENA

School will be over soon. I'll go and pick up the girls. (*exits*)

*CARMELA is breastfeeding the baby. NEVA takes it all in for a
moment.*

NEVA

My God, the way they go at it.

CARMELA

They don't know what they want from each other. I'll tell
you one thing though, I'm going to need her here. When
this boy is old enough, I'm going to have to work. Who's
going to take care of my kids? I need her here.

NEVA
Maybe that's not such a good idea.

CARMELA
We'll never make it otherwise. Io debbo lavorare. I have to
work. I can't depend on Silvio for money. Because of his
pride as a carpenter, he walks out on jobs. He has no
concept of money. He earns it, and then it disappears. I
have to manage it, and he's not earning enough to move
forward here.

NEVA
Why didn't you tell me you had rheumatic fever? I worry
about you. I want you to come to the hospital for a full
examination. I'll set it up today.

CARMELA
I'm fine, really.

NEVA
Carmela, don't go and sacrifice your life, your health
because those two can't get along. You shouldn't be caught
in the middle of their war.

CARMELA
He's my husband, what are you asking me to do?

NEVA
You have to put your foot down now, before it's too late.
You have to demand some peace in this house, or it will
never come. Think of your health.

CARMELA
Do you think I just let things go? Trying to be a peace-
maker between them is like eating pizza with a spoon. It
gets you no where.

NEVA
You're young, Carmela, you have your whole life in front of
you. Listen to me. I see lots of men come through the
emergency ward. I get to see so many problems. Drunks,

accidents because of drunken husbands, women beaten
because of drunken husbands.

CARMELA

My husband is not a drunk.

NEVA

My point is, that even after the women have been hit, and
the husband is at their side in the emergency ward, they
just let it go. They get treated for their wounds, and then
they go home and it begins the cycle all over again. Why?
Because the wife allows the behaviour. She does nothing to
stop it.

CARMELA

Silvio doesn't hit me.

NEVA

I know that. But this bickering back and forth, if you don't
put your foot down, they will keep doing it. Think of your
children.

CARMELA

That's all I do, Neva. Everything I do is for this little boy
and my two girls. You mustn't put your modern thoughts
on our Italian ways here.

NEVA

What is so Italian about letting your husband and mother-
in-law get away with such behaviour? It's nonsense, I'm
telling you.

CARMELA

Neva, please ... I can handle it ...

NEVA

They've made great progress now. Medical science has
gone to places we couldn't have imagined just ten years
ago. They have doctors now, doctors who study behaviour.

CARMELA

Are you talking about one of those head doctors?

NEVA

They call them psychiatrists. Instead of treating a broken
limb, or a sore throat, they treat your mind.

CARMELA

I know what a *psichiatra* is. Are you saying I should go see
one?

NEVA

No ... heaven no ... I'm talking about Silvio. Listen to me,
Carmela, there are lots of wounded soldiers out there.
They come home from battle, and they are not right up
here. They need to understand why they are still in pain.
They've experienced things we cannot possibly imagine.
Keeping it in ... not talking about it is not a healthy thing.
Does he talk about the war with you? With his mother?

CARMELA

No.

NEVA

He needs to unload ... He's full of rage ... he needs proper
medical care. It's the only way he can survive himself.

CARMELA

You don't know him. I do. He doesn't like to be
contradicted. And that's all his mother does. Is contradict
him.

NEVA

This is more complicated than you think.

CARMELA

No it's not. The last thing I'm going to suggest is for my
Silvio to go see a head doctor.

NEVA

You want me to do it? Carmela, you want me to do it?

CARMELA

(*crying*) No. My Silvio doesn't need one. I can take care of
him.

NEVA

I'm sorry. I didn't mean ... oh, please forgive me ... (*She smothers CARMELA in kisses.*) Please ... you mean the world to me. I meant no harm. I've said what I said. I will speak no more of it. I'm sorry. Is there anything I can do?

CARMELA

You can stop kissing me.

They share a laugh.

NEVA

Oh, Carmela ... Please don't think bad of me. I'm trying to help. (*pause*) I'll go. I should get to work now. Ciao. I'll see you tonight. (*exits*)

CARMELA keeps breastfeeding the baby. She kisses his head ever so gently.

CARMELA

You're my little prince, you're my little prince ... what are we going to do with all this confusion here? I'll protect you. Don't you worry about that. I always will. (*pause, singing softly*)

	(*English translation*)
Giro Giro Tondo	*Turn, turn around*
Quando è bello il mondo!	*How beautiful the world is!*
Cento, cinquanta,	*One-hundred fifty,*
La gallina canta.	*The chicken sings.*
Canta da sola,	*She sings by herself,*
Non vuole andare a scuola.	*She doesn't want to go to school.*
Ma la scuola è tanto bella.	*But the school is so pretty.*
Canta canta gallinella!	*Sing, sing little chicken.*

She continues breastfeeding the child as the lights fade slowly to black.

Scene Three

It's just a little past midnight. All is quiet when screaming is heard from inside the house. It is SILVIO having a nightmare. We hear the sounds of little girls crying for their mother. We hear FILOMENA trying to calm them down. Now the infant is crying too.

SILVIO
(*off-stage*) GET DOWN! GET DOWN! DIO PERDONAMI! DIO PERDONAMI!

CARMELA
(*overlapping*) Silvio ... Silvio ... calmati. It's okay. I'm here ... I'm here ... stay calm ... calmati ... no one's going to hurt you. Sshhh ... it's okay ...

We hear shouting from the lane: "Will you people shut up! We're trying to sleep here!" "Retournez chez vous mon tabernac! C'est un monde de fou!" SILVIO comes storming into the yard. He's doing up his zipper. He seems lost and very dazed and confused. He tries to compose himself. The girls in the house are quiet now. The infant is still crying.

CARMELA
(*enters*) Come inside ...

SILVIO
Get me my shoes.

CARMELA
Silvio, please ...

SILVIO
Just get me my shoes!

CARMELA exits. SILVIO is still breathing hard. CARMELA enters with his shoes, FILOMENA is following behind.

CARMELA
It's okay, Silvio, you had a bad dream.

FILOMENA
Is he okay?

CARMELA
Ma, please! Go check on the girls. (*FILOMENA exits.
CARMELA approaches SILVIO very calmly and touches him very
gently.*) Come inside.

> *DAVE comes running into the yard. He's dressed in civilian
> clothes.*

CARMELA
It's fine, Dave. Go back home.

DAVE
You scared my mother half to death. What happened?

> *More shouting from the lane: "Faites ta job come du monde.
> Avec ce crisse de wop la je peux pas dormire!"*

DAVE
(*shouts back*) Jacques, calme toi! Je va regler ça. Tout est
correcte.

> *NEVA appears at the upper window.*

NEVA
What's going on out there?

DAVE
Neva, go to sleep. I'll handle it.

NEVA
I'm coming down.

DAVE
(*sternly*) You stay in your house. I'll take care of it.

> *NEVA exits.*

DAVE
Silvio. You alright? Anything I can do? Come on ... I'm
here as a friend ...

FILOMENA
(*enters*) Carmela, the baby's hungry.

CARMELA
Dave, will you stay with him? (*to FILOMENA*) How are the girls?

FILOMENA
They're scared.

CARMELA and FILOMENA exit. DAVE touches SILVIO. With lightning speed SILVIO grabs him.

DAVE
Easy, there now, Silvio. Take it easy ... it's me ... Dave ... your friend ... Do you see me? It's me Dave. Dave Damonti.

SILVIO's leg buckles, he sits and rubs his leg.

DAVE
You okay? (*pause*) Spoke to Martino. There won't be any charges. You won't have to worry about him anymore.

The two men are silent, as DAVE gives SILVIO his space.

SILVIO
It's late, Dave, go home.

DAVE
Don't worry about it.

SILVIO
You're a good boy, Dave. (*pause*) I feel a little ... you know ... about this ... I stopped having the nightmares for a long time. When I was in Belgium I slept like a baby. No nightmares.

DAVE
What happened?

SILVIO
I don't know, I came to this country ... my mother ...

DAVE

Your mother … don't worry about your mother.

SILVIO

You don't know that woman.

DAVE

She's like all the other Italian moms. They just want to take care of the family.

SILVIO

She took care of me. She took care of me real good.

DAVE

Of course she did …

SILVIO

When I was a prisoner of war in England …

DAVE

That must've been tough.

SILVIO

My time there wasn't all that bad. The camp was in a small town called Reading. During the day the Italians would be escorted to various work details under guard. A farm, a road way. And sometimes on an estate.

DAVE

You mean those famous British estates?

SILVIO

You know how big those estates are? All that land? Someone has to take care of it. The grass. The bushes. The tennis courts. The apple trees. (*pause*) The apple trees.

DAVE

So they put you to work as gardeners, caretakers?

SILVIO

They sure did. And we welcomed it. Took us away from the dreariness of the camp. One day we were assigned to this estate. The Hodgkin estate. I remember when we arrived.

My life changed forever that day. There was this young
woman who would watch us work. She owned the estate.

DAVE
She owned the estate?

SILVIO
Well, she was orphaned. She inherited the estate, with a
team of servants around her.

DAVE
What was her name?

SILVIO
Mary Louise. (*pause*) On the fourth day, she was talking to
one of the guards. The next thing you know, she points to
me. I thought I was in trouble. A guard comes over to me
and says that I am to escort Mary Louise to the apple
orchard. So on this lorry we go.

DAVE
Lorry?

SILVIO
Truck. That's what the British call it. A lorry. And she's
driving.

DAVE
You two alone?

SILVIO
I know it sounds crazy. So we arrive at the apple orchard,
and she just sat there talking to me. I didn't know much
English at the time. So I smiled and nodded my head. And
then it happened. She took my hand, and said, "You. You
are not like the others."

DAVE
What did she mean by that?

SILVIO
I didn't know. I didn't have the words to talk. I couldn't
speak her language. I'm about to climb out of the truck

when she holds me back. I thought I was being set up. You know ... for an execution. And who would know? I mean this was a girl of high standing and she's touching a prisoner. That was forbidden. But she touched me. And then she kissed me.

DAVE

She kissed you? What did you do?

SILVIO

I froze. I thought I was being tested. Some British way of testing the prisoners. But there was no one around. No one was watching. She kissed me again. And still I froze. My eyes wide open. She then gently covered my eyes with her soft clean hands. And kissed me again. Now I'm totally lost, and I kissed her back. What else was I supposed to do?

DAVE

You made out with a British girl?

SILVIO

It was more than that. You see. She convinced the commander of the camp to keep the prisoners on her estate every once in a while. There was this back house, a small little place big enough for about a dozen prisoners. They left us there with a few guards. On the first night, just as I was ready to sleep, a guard orders me out. He escorts me to a back entrance where a servant was waiting for me. I was invited in and shown to the dining room, where Mary Louise was waiting for me. I had dinner with her, and didn't leave the house till early the next morning.

DAVE

You slept there? You slept ... I mean ... did you ... ?

SILVIO

It went on for three years.

DAVE

You had an affair with a British woman for three years?

SILVIO
She taught me how to speak. I taught her opera. She taught me some English history, I taught her how to cook.

DAVE
Were you in love?

SILVIO
The war came to an end, and I had to go back. She promised me that she would get me back to England and we were to start a life together.

DAVE
You were going to marry her?

SILVIO
We were in love.

DAVE is stunned by this story. He is trying to piece together what he's just heard.

DAVE
But you never married her. What happened?

SILVIO
I got back to Italy ... she ...

DAVE
She never wrote you? Silvio. She did write you. What happened? My God, your life would've went in a totally different direction. You wouldn't have married Carmela, you wouldn't be here ... but your marriage—Do you love Carmela?

SILVIO
What?

DAVE
I mean what you just told me ... Do you love Carmela?

SILVIO
(*erupting*) How can you ask me that! Get out of here!

DAVE
Silvio, we're talking …

Shouting from the lane: "Do you have any idea what fucking time it is? Why don't you play more opera so we can all enjoy the music! Fuck your wife while you're at it too!"

SILVIO
That son-of-a-bitch! I'm going to take care of this right now! (*He storms inside the house. He comes back out carrying a full bottle of wine, and then exits the yard.*)

DAVE
Where are you going?

CARMELA
(*enters with the baby*) Where you going with that bottle? Dave, please go after him.

NEVA enters the yard.

NEVA
Carmela …

DAVE
Silvio! Silvio, wait! (*exits*)

NEVA
This can't go on.

CARMELA
Don't you think I know that! He's impossible to talk to!

FILOMENA
(*enters the yard*) Where did he go?

CARMELA
Ma, please, go back inside.

NEVA
Don't make things worse. The girls need you.

FILOMENA
He's paying for all the damage he's done. And you,
Carmela, you don't help at all. You can't go changing
things around him. He likes his food spicy, you make it
mild. He plays cards, you're always complaining. Let him
have his way.

CARMELA
I'm trying to raise three children. I can't be worrying about
how much spice I put in the beans.

FILOMENA
You're not giving him enough attention.

CARMELA
What do you mean by that?

FILOMENA
You know what I mean.

NEVA
Mrs. Rosato, your pride was wounded, don't take it out on
Carmela. Your son needs help, he's needed help from the
beginning.

FILOMENA
You have nothing to tell me about how to raise a son.
Nothing. I did my part.

CARMELA
And I'm trying to do mine. But I can't do it with you in the
way. You've meddled with his life one too many times.

FILOMENA
What do you mean by that?

CARMELA
You know what I mean. Remember England?

FILOMENA
I will not be spoken to that way. (*She takes it in and exits into
the house.*)

CARMELA

She can go to hell for all I care. My God, what did I get myself into?

NEVA

Just give it some time.

CARMELA

I've been married for nine years, how much time does it take? I'm trying, Neva. I'm trying. I don't know where to go with him. We were so good in Belgium.

NEVA

Was Filomena there with you?

CARMELA

No it was just me, Silvio, and the girls.

NEVA

There you go. And his behaviour wasn't like this?

CARMELA

No. He was easy to talk to. We'd go out ... he'd make love to me any opportunity he had. He played with the girls ... then we went back to Italy and his mother.

NEVA

He resents everything from his past. He feels guilty. He's beating himself up because of his past.

CARMELA

These nightmares ... I can't imagine what he went through.

NEVA

He needs help. He needs to see a doctor. Now, what's this thing about England? I heard Silvio say ... to Filomena, what she did to him twelve years ago. What did she do to him? Twelve years ago, that was after the war. What did she do?

DAVE enters. He's quiet and a little stunned.

CARMELA

We'll talk about it later with four eyes. (*to DAVE*) What's wrong? Where's my Silvio?

DAVE

Eh? Oh. Uh ... he'll be coming. He's just taking a walk down the block. May I hold the baby?

CARMELA

He's sleeping.

DAVE

May I just hold him for a second? They're so peaceful.

CARMELA hands the baby to DAVE. He ever so gently brings the baby up to his cheek. He kisses the baby. He hands the baby to CARMELA.

NEVA

What happened?

DAVE

It was the strangest thing I've ever seen.

NEVA

Dave, snap out of it! What the hell happened?

CARMELA

Neva, take the baby, I'm going to go find him.

DAVE

No, don't do that. Let him be. He needs to ...

SILVIO enters. His presence makes everyone stay quiet. SILVIO approaches CARMELA and kisses the baby.

CARMELA

Why doesn't everybody just go home.

NEVA

Silvio. Listen to me. I want you to come with me to the hospital. There is a department there ... doctors who take care of wounded war veterans. You can talk to them. They can help you.

SILVIO suddenly picks up his hammer and whacks the top of his work table. He then grabs the work table and topples it over. He continues hammering at the work table, taking out all his rage on the object. This is frightening and it arrests everyone in the yard.

SILVIO

You people think you know me? You people ... at the end of the day ... are such small petty-minded little pieces of nothing. One bad dream, and you have to blow it all out of proportion.

NEVA

Look at the way you're behaving.

SILVIO

Is this what you want, Carmela? Is this what you want? We were so good in Belgium.

CARMELA

So what happened?

SILVIO

I DON'T KNOW WHAT HAPPENED! I DON'T KNOW WHAT FUCKING HAPPENED! But don't stand there and listen to this nosy good-for-nothing whore-bitch!

FILOMENA

(*enters*) Dave. Go home to your wife. She'll be worried. Go to her. You people are just complicating everything. Now go home both of you.

SILVIO

Here she is. This is the one who can solve everything. Here's the one who has all the answers.

FILOMENA

Oh, son, you will live to regret how you talk to me. The venom that comes out of your mouth ...

SILVIO
Nothing good can come out of me. I'm poison to those
around me. Dave here doesn't know if he's coming or
going ... Neva meddles where it's not her business, you
despise anything that's good, and my wife is too ignorant to
know the difference.

NEVA
Silvio, I'm sorry if I overstepped my bounds, but Carmela
has nothing to do with it.

SILVIO
Good then. You can all leave. And never come back here
again.

FILOMENA
I don't know what's inside your belly, but you better pray it
doesn't kill you.

SILVIO
I'M ALREADY DEAD, MA! CAN'T YOU SEE! I'M ALREADY A
DEAD MAN! AND YOU KILLED ME! Now, listen good, Ma.
You go inside and pack your bags. You pack a suitcase,
because you're leaving this house. I'm putting you on a
boat back to Italy, and you can go live with your daughter.
You're leaving my house, and I never want to see you again.

*FILOMENA exits into the house. SILVIO crosses out onto the side
entrance and comes right back out with a work-light. He steps
inside the house momentarily to run an electrical extension
cord. There's nothing more to say, so DAVE motions to NEVA
that they leave. NEVA gently approaches CARMELA. She kisses
her and exits.*

SILVIO
I can't be with people. I don't know how to be with people.
I don't have anything more to give. I'm empty inside ...
You're looking at a dead man. I'm no good to any of you.
Least of all the children. They should not be around me.

77

CARMELA

Don't say that. Let's get some sleep, and all will be well in the morning.

SILVIO

Don't you understand? We can't go on like this.

CARMELA

It's only been two months.

SILVIO

It won't get any better. All I do is hurt people. And that's not what's in my heart.

CARMELA

I know, it's that mouth of yours, what comes out of it …

SILVIO

I'm going to finish this table for you.

CARMELA

Silvio …

SILVIO

Don't argue with me. I'm going to build you this table. I'm going to build this table because I need to know that I can do some good on this earth. When I build something, I know it's good. And nobody gets hurt. When my children see this table, they will know I tried to make things last. To make things good.

CARMELA

It's past midnight … why are you doing this?

SILVIO

Put the child to sleep. This night air can't be good for him.

CARMELA

Silvio …

SILVIO

Just do as I say and don't contradict me.

CARMELA exits. SILVIO quietly picks up his hammer. He crosses to the unfinished table, and looks at it for a moment. He picks up a piece of cut wood and begins to hammer in the first slat of the table top. A different voice from the lane is heard shouting: "Go to sleep you fucking wop! This is a civilized country!" SILVIO takes his hammer and violently rushes to the edge of the yard. For a moment it looks like he's going to fling it across the lane in the direction of the shouting, but holds it back. It is now quiet in the lane. SILVIO looks out, his stare is deadly and angry. The lights fade slowly to black.

Silvio and Carmela on their wedding day, Italy, November 27, 1948.

Silvio and Carmela later on their wedding day, Italy, November 27, 1948.

Top: Silvio in Belgium, 1955.
Bottom: Silvio and Carmela in Belgium, 1955.

Top: Carmela and Lucia Liliana in Belgium, 1955.
Bottom: Carmela in Italy, 1955.

Top: Carmela in Italy, circa 1955.
Bottom: Filomena, Maria, Carmela and Lucia Liliana, Italy, mid 1954.

Maria and Lucia Liliana, Italy, 1956.

Carmela, Lucia Liliana, Filomena and Maria, Italy, 1956.

Maria and Lucia Liliana, in Montreal, 1958.

Act Two

Scene One

Late morning of the following day. Scraps of wood lie about the yard. A huge tarp hangs over the work area.
NEVA is in the kitchen sipping coffee, and folding clean diapers. DAVE is there pacing, he is dressed in full uniform.

DAVE

So last night ... nothing happened?

NEVA

Nothing at all. He worked on the table and went to sleep. Me and Mike watched from the window. He has such focus when he works. It's astonishing.

DAVE

I don't understand this. Strange man, that Silvio. I'll tell you that.

NEVA

Why do you say that?

DAVE

Last night. Silvio and the neighbour ... I really thought Silvio was going to kill him. Then I saw the bottle of wine in his hand. The neighbour goes: "What are you doing here? Do you know what time it is? Do you want me to call the police? I'll have you arrested."

NEVA

What did Silvio say?

DAVE

That's the thing. He took out his hand to shake. All he said
was: "Buona sera, I'm Silvio Rosato. This is for you." He
hands him the bottle of wine. And then Silvio just stared at
him. He gave him this look. I've never seen anything like it.
He put the fear of God in that neighbour. A look that
could kill. But it was more than that. This look ... oh, I
don't know how Carmela does it.

NEVA

The neighbour said nothing?

DAVE

Not a word. Silvio gave him this look. It was like he didn't
care about himself. This look said: "What do you think you
can do to me that hasn't already been done?" I'll say this, if
that man, the neighbour, wasn't healthy, he would've had a
heart attack.

NEVA

Just by a look?

DAVE

It was more than a look, Neva. It was ... not of this world.
Like he was transported somewhere ... to a place only he
knows how to get to. And that place is dark. It's very dark.
He scared the living daylights out of that guy. Anyone else
would've clocked the neighbour right in the kisser. But not
Silvio. He disarmed that man's stupidity with an act of
kindness. He offered him his wine. And then that look.
Carmela lives with that look every day. How does she do it?

NEVA

Let this thing go, I don't want Carmela upset anymore.
Okay? We'll talk later with four eyes.

DAVE

What?

CARMELA enters the kitchen with her new self-made dress on.

NEVA

Look at you.

CARMELA

Tell me if it all looks even. (*She stands on a chair.*) What do you think, Dave?

DAVE

I like it. It gives you a nice line.

CARMELA

What about the breasts?

DAVE

Carmela …

CARMELA

One day, when Luciano is a grown man, I'm going to tell him what a fuss it was to breastfeed him out in the open.

NEVA

It's fine, Carmela.

CARMELA

(*jumps off the chair and twirls around*) It's not too high?

NEVA

It's perfect. You look spectacular in it. All you have to do now is make sure Silvio doesn't jump all over you.

DAVE

Where is he?

CARMELA

He went to get his picture taken for Immigration.

DAVE

Is he okay?

CARMELA

Who knows. What can I do? I have children to feed.

NEVA

What about Filomena? Is she leaving?

CARMELA

The only one who can stop her is Silvio. If he doesn't say
something, she's going to leave. (*The phone rings.*) Pronto. I
mean ... hello. Yes. What? O Dio! Is he okay? I'll tell him as
soon as he gets in. (*hangs up*) It's just like Silvio said. The
floor came crashing down. One of the carpenters is in the
hospital. Broken back, ribs ... That was Martino. He wants
Silvio back on the job.

DAVE

That's good, Carmela, he's gotta get back to work, because
last night ... we can't have any more of this in the backyard,
understand?

NEVA

Dave ...

DAVE

No, you listen to me now. I'm thinking of my own mother's
health. Every time Silvio erupts, her heart skips a few beats.
I can't have that. She rented this place to you in good faith.
I'm talking to you as a landlord now. Understand?

CARMELA

What do you want me to do?

DAVE

Things have to change here, Carmela. They have to change
now. I might not be at the station when the next call comes
in, and if they send over a couple of French cops, he'll be
cuffed and brought in. Is that what you want?

NEVA

Okay ... you said what you said, now go to work, and we'll
take it from here.

CARMELA

No, wait. Stay for lunch. Please. Silvio will be back soon.
Give him a chance to apologize.

DAVE
He's going to apologize for last night?

CARMELA
I know he will. But he won't apologize with words.

DAVE
He won't?

CARMELA
No. Never. I've never seen him do it. He'll do it with his actions. He'll fix something for you. Or maybe he'll give you something, he'll buy that extra piece of fruit, he'll take me for an ice cream. But he'll never come out and say: I'm sorry.

DAVE
He's never said I'm sorry to you?

CARMELA
No. Never.

DAVE
But if he doesn't say it, how do you know for sure he's apologizing?

CARMELA
I know. Believe me, I know. Maybe with you, he'll give you something. Please.

FILOMENA enters the kitchen.

FILOMENA
All the way to school, Maria was complaining because she wants a new dress.

NEVA
I can get you more material.

CARMELA
You've already done enough.

NEVA
Anything for those little girls. What about Liliana?

FILOMENA

Liliana is fine. She doesn't complain about her clothes. It's Maria you have to be careful about. She's a very curious little girl. (*She hands NEVA an envelope.*) Here's some money. I want you to get me a ticket to go back home. And I don't want to go through Nuova York again.

NEVA

You won't have to. They'll have a train to Halifax. From there you'll get on a ship.

FILOMENA

Good. That's fine. Now be a good girl, and get me the first ticket out of here.

NEVA

Mrs. Rosato ...

FILOMENA

It's best for all of us. I'll go back and live with my daughter. I won't live where I'm not wanted.

The baby is heard crying. CARMELA exits.

FILOMENA

Neva, I'm not asking for much, Dave, you listen to this ... You must promise me both that you will help Silvio. Take care of him. Love Silvio like a brother. Carmela ... she'll need you too. And don't worry about me. I still have my daughter. She will take care of me in my final years. I should have never come here.

The phone rings.

CARMELA

(*off-stage*) Can you get that, Ma!

FILOMENA

(*on phone*) Pronto. What? I don't understand.

NEVA

You have to say hello. Here we say hello.

FILOMENA
(*on phone*) Hello. No, he's not here. Wait a minute ... Ma-why you have to use this kind of language? Fuck-a this ... and a fuck-a that ... eh fuckayou too. Cazzo ...

CARMELA
(*rushes into the kitchen and grabs the phone*) Ma ...

FILOMENA
It's Luigi. Enrico's cousin's brother.

CARMELA
(*on phone*) Hello. Yes, Luigi. How is he? Both legs? Madonna! How is he going to walk? Yes. Yes. He'll be here soon. He will. I'll tell him. (*hangs up the phone*) Enrico, Luigi's brother's cousin broke his back, and both legs on that construction site.

DAVE
(*still thinking*) Enrico's cousin's brother. If the brother is the cousin, then that makes it Enrico's cousin.

CARMELA
It's the same person.

DAVE
That's what I'm saying.

CARMELA
But we don't know his brother.

DAVE
It's still the cousin.

CARMELA
Whose cousin?

DAVE
Enrico's

CARMELA
That's right.

FILOMENA
Why do you have to make things so confusing?

DAVE
I'm not. I'm just saying ... for simplicity ... Enrico has a cousin, and that cousin has a brother. If they are brothers, then they are both cousins to Enrico.

FILOMENA
That's what she said.

NEVA
Are they related?

DAVE
They are if they're brothers.

CARMELA
Enrico doesn't have a brother.

DAVE
No, but he has a cousin.

FILOMENA
What does this have to do with Luigi?

CARMELA
He just called. On behalf of Enrico, his brother's cousin.

DAVE
Which makes it his cousin.

CARMELA
Oooofa! Why is this so complicated to you? Does Enrico have a brother?

FILOMENA
Ma-what do I know? This poor boy here doesn't know how to follow a conversation.

SILVIO enters the kitchen dressed in a suit.

CARMELA
Silvio, Luigi called. I told him you'd call back.

SILVIO

I'll call him later. (*He opens a cupboard and takes out a small wooden box.*) Dave, you want to play cards tonight?

DAVE

My shift ends late.

SILVIO

I'll be waiting for you. We'll call over Pasquale, and Guido.

DAVE

I don't like Guido. He cheats.

SILVIO

He cheats when he plays?

DAVE

I know it.

SILVIO

So we'll call ... what's his name? You know ... what's his name? The son of Tony's sister.

DAVE

You mean Tony's nephew?

SILVIO

It's the same person.

DAVE

Isn't it easier to just say Tony's nephew?

SILVIO

Yes, but I don't know his sister.

DAVE

Forget it. I know who you're talking about. His name is Aldo.

SILVIO

Yes. That's the guy.

DAVE

I'll see him later.

CARMELA

Silvio, they need you back on the job. Why don't you call Luigi back? You can start working again.

SILVIO

Carmela, please ... I'm busy. And I hate using the phone.

DAVE

Why do you hate using the phone?

SILVIO

Because when I talk to someone, I want to make eye contact. That's the only way I can tell if that person is an honest one. (*He takes out a letter from his suit pocket, and hands it to FILOMENA.*) Here, give this letter to my sister. Dave, I have something for you. (*He hands him the wooden box.*) I made this for you. When you come home at night, you can put your badge in here, your watch, whatever you want.

DAVE

You made this?

The phone rings.

CARMELA

(*on phone*) Pronto! Mannaggia la miseria! Hello. Yes ... yes ... who ... Martino. Yes he's right here. Silvio.

SILVIO

What does he want? (*He grabs the phone.*) Yes. Yes. Enrico is in the hospital. I warned you. Yes. Yes. Ah. I see. Good, good. Now you listen to me. You got lucky this time that nobody got killed. Those houses stand on unstable ground. The basements need drain wells ... yes ... a drain system. Understand? If you want me back at work, I have conditions. Conditions. Yes you heard me. One: I need three carpenters under my direction. Not two, three. Two: When I work, you can't be on the site. I don't care if you're the contractor. I don't want you near me when I work. Three: I want more money. Four: Enrico is in the hospital.

Yes. I want you to pay his hospital bills. That's right, Martino. Those are my conditions. You want your houses built, you know where to find me. (*hangs up*)

CARMELA
Silvio, we have no money coming in, just go back to work.

SILVIO
Carmela, please, I'm handling it.

FILOMENA
These are not the times to ask for more money.

SILVIO
What do you care, you're leaving.

FILOMENA
Listen to your wife, go back to work. How do you expect to feed your children?

CARMELA
Ma, please ...

FILOMENA
You hate me, that's fine, but think of your family. You can dishonour me, you don't have to dishonour your wife and children.

SILVIO
Good-bye, Ma. (*crosses into the backyard*)

FILOMENA
(*follows him out*) You could turn your back on me, but you will have to live with the shame you brought on to my name with what you did. I want my apology before I leave.

SILVIO
You won't let it go, ah, Ma. You just can't let it go.

FILOMENA
I'll never let it go. Never. I'm going back to Italy so I can have my life back. I want my honour back. You hear me! I want it back!

SILVIO

What about my apology? What about the apology I'm owed
for what you did to me.

CARMELA

Silvio, please ...

*CARMELA crosses into the backyard with DAVE and NEVA
following behind.*

SILVIO

No, Carmela. This woman has to learn to mind her own
business. Go ahead, tell them what you did to me. After the
war. Tell them about Mary Louise. Remember her, Ma?
Back in England ... that woman I had, who was waiting for
me. Tell them what you did.

DAVE

Silvio ... please ...

SILVIO

No, Dave ... you wanted to know what happened. We were
to be married. When they released the prisoners ... I got
back to Italy. I kept waiting for Mary Louise to call on me.
Six months turned into a year, and a year turned into two.
Ask her. She'll tell you. Or don't you want to admit to your
poisonous act.

FILOMENA

I did it to help you.

SILVIO

HOW DID YOU HELP ME! HOW? You see, Dave ... I was
working one day on this farm. And one of the workers tells
me of mail that was coming to the house. Almost twice a
week. From England. We never got mail. Not in a little
town like that. I was getting mail. From England. And when
the mail came, I never knew about it. Why is that, Dave?
Why? My mother. My mother would intercept the letters
and burn them. Why, Ma? Why did you do that? Mary
Louise never knew. She never knew. And I never heard

from her again. This is what she did to me. This is the woman you are all defending here. And you have the face to question my honour.

FILOMENA

I did it to protect you. That was not your world. You never would've survived there.

SILVIO

IT WAS NOT YOUR DECISION TO MAKE! It was my life! You played with my life! I could've had it made. I could've been a prince there. And now I'm in the hell you placed me in!

CARMELA

(*erupting*) ENOUGH! The both of you! I'm not going to have this anymore! Do you understand? Both of you can go to hell for all I care, because I am not going to take this anymore! Why does it always have to be a fight with the two of you? Why? You two are the most selfish people I have ever met. It's always me me me. It's never about the other person. WE HAVE CHILDREN IN THIS HOUSE! DO BOTH OF YOU UNDERSTAND! MY CHILDREN! And they are not going to be surrounded by this hell you are both in.

FILOMENA

What have I done?

CARMELA

SHUT UP! SHUT UP! And let me have my peace. You regretful vengeful old bag. Your son went through hell, and you can't give him a minute of understanding. You had a hard time of it in your life. You want us to feel sorry for you because your stupid, disgusting, disloyal husband left you for another woman. There … I feel sorry for you and so does the entire world. What can you do with that? What? Can you make your life any better? Can you?

NEVA

Carmela, please stay calm …

CARMELA

I'm not going to stay calm! I'm not going to stay calm! This is my home, and I will set the orders here. And you will learn to live with it, or you can leave. I don't need you. My daughters don't need you. And my little boy doesn't need you. I can handle this all on my own. And if you think I can't, just watch me. Your son survived a war, Ma! He survived because he wanted to live. He survived because he cared. Why can't you understand that! Why? Why must you live this life of pity? Why didn't you just re-marry? You could've done that. Maybe another man would have made you happy. Maybe another man could've satisfied you in bed ... and maybe things would've been different. But you didn't do that. Did you? You played the role of the saint. You had your opportunity, you made your choice, live with it. And I won't have you take my opportunity away from me. This is my life you're playing with here.

SILVIO

Carmela ...

CARMELA

Don't touch me! Don't you dare touch me! (*She's now really lost it. She begins to hyperventilate. She finds the strength to move on.*) I am your wife. And you will listen to me. Your stupid useless war is over! Do you understand that? It's over. It's been over for twelve years! HOW MUCH LONGER DOES THIS HAVE TO GO ON! I am not your enemy. Your mother is not your enemy. Neva and Dave are not your enemies! Learn to live with the fact that people love you. They want to love you. Why do you push us away with your anger? Why? Why? We have children, Silvio! We have children! Is this the world you want them to live in! Is it? Answer me! (*pause*) What are you feeling now! What is it? You want to hit me! You can't take what should've been said the day we were married. You think I'm here to be servant to your tragic life? Is that what you think this is about? Because if that's what you want, then you didn't marry a wife. No, sir. I am not going to be a slave to your self-serving pathetic anger.

NEVA

Carmela …

CARMELA

(*She is trying to catch her breath. Her breathing is laboured.*) I … will not … have this … in my home anymore. I've been patient. I've held it in. But now here it is. You decide if you want to be loved. You make that decision. You decide what you expect from me. And then you think about what you want for yourself. This fantasy you keep living … about what could've been or should've been … with that woman in England … your mother burnt the letters. Okay. Why didn't you write her? Why didn't you go back there and explain to her what your mother did? Why didn't you? (*to FILOMENA*) What you did was pathetic! Disgusting! I would never do that to a child of mine. (*to SILVIO*) But what you did was worse. You never let go of the apron. Now live with it.

CARMELA exits into the house. They all stay silent, unable to say anything. CARMELA comes back out with the baby and places him in the carriage.

CARMELA

I'm taking my boy for a walk. I'm going to play with him in the park. I'm going to tickle him all over and I want to hear him laugh. When he's hungry, I'm going to breastfeed him out in the open. I don't care what the law is. I don't care what the neighbours think. I don't care who is watching. This is my son. And I will nurse him as I see fit. Then I'm going to pick up my little girls from school. I'm going to walk with them and buy them an ice cream. I'm going to smother them with hugs and kisses. I'm going to make them understand that no matter what happens in life, they will always have their mother. Now, I want you to take a look at your son. Go ahead. Take a look at him. And tell him if the world you lived in is what you want him to have.

Go ahead. Tell this little creature. Tell him. (*SILVIO does not make a move.*) You may have affected the little girls. And I will do my best to let them know that they will be protected from you. But I will be damned if this little boy is touched by your anger. Neva, let's go.

NEVA
Carmela …

CARMELA
March!

CARMELA steers the baby carriage off and exits with NEVA following behind. DAVE turns to SILVIO and FILOMENA, but decides to say nothing. He exits. SILVIO and FILOMENA stand there looking at each other as the lights fade slowly to black.

Later that night. SILVIO is in the backyard sitting looking out. DAVE is with him dressed in full uniform.

SILVIO

You think she'll come back?

DAVE

One thing I know about Carmela is that she loves you. She loves you in ways that cannot be measured. I'm telling you this as a friend ... I know what you think when you see me in my uniform.

SILVIO

I have great respect for you. I just don't want you to be pushed around, that's all.

DAVE

They don't push me around. You mustn't let your pride get in the way here.

SILVIO

I don't need you to lecture me.

DAVE

Carmela was bound to let it out. She had to. She's put up with way too much. She needs some room to breathe. You and your mother must come to an understanding, or Carmela won't make it, Silvio. She won't. Did you see her breathing?

SILVIO

How can I ever look at her the same again?

DAVE

You'll find a way. You should be happy that she stood up to you, and your mother. She's no pushover, Carmela. Did you want a wife that just says yes to your every command? She gave you her love the day she said yes to your proposal of marriage. Now you have to show her that you want her.

That you need her. You have to apologize to her. She's your wife.

SILVIO

I've done nothing wrong. Not to her.

DAVE

Yes you did. You brought her into your world, and only you know how dark it is in there. You brought her there, and now you brought her here, and now you have to tell her that it's going to be fine in this new world. That the old is done with.

SILVIO

Words, Dave, it's all words ... easier said than done.

DAVE

I know it is, but what choice do you have? Just give her the words, Silvio. Let her know.

SILVIO

All my life seems to be spent around a table. Eating, playing cards, playing with the baby ... Remember one thing, Dave. The kitchen table is the throne of the poor. It's where all of life's decisions are made. It was at the kitchen table where I asked Carmela's father for his permission to marry her. And it was at the kitchen table where I asked her to take a walk with me where I then proposed. The kitchen table. Whoever commands the table, commands the house. You remember that.

DAVE

I will.

SILVIO

When she first caught my eye ... She had that smile ... you know ... it was generous ... it lit up a room ... and yet there was a shyness to her. She had a simple dress, and she was wearing these sandals. She had the cutest feet ... you should've seen, not like the other girls, she took care of herself. When I approached her ... I gave her this ... (*He suddenly rises, and exits.*)

DAVE
Where you going?

NEVA enters the yard with the baby in the carriage.

NEVA
Was that Silvio?

DAVE
Yeah, he just ran off.

NEVA
Where to?

DAVE
I don't know.

FILOMENA enters and crosses to the carriage to look over the baby.

FILOMENA
Neva, where's Carmela?

NEVA
She's putting the girls to sleep.

FILOMENA
Back in my day a wife's place was by her husband. They have children, and children need a home.

DAVE
You have this all wrong, Mrs. Rosato. Carmela showed some independent spirit, and there's nothing wrong in that. You can't smother her free will.

FILOMENA
We have free will, but we obey the laws of God and the Church.

NEVA
Maybe the Church is wrong. Did you ever think of that?

FILOMENA

How can the Church be wrong? It's the instrument of God. If you believe in him, then you must obey his laws. You're not a godfearing woman are you?

NEVA

I didn't say that. My problem is with the Church. Come on, when your husband left you, he broke God's law. It's written right there ... a man ... a husband ... must not desire another woman. Your husband broke his law. You could've moved on with your life. You didn't because somehow the Church made you believe that if you did, you were in the wrong. Well. That's not what God says. So how did the Church help you?

FILOMENA

I did move on with my life. I saved my children.

NEVA

And that's a noble thing. That was a courageous act on your part. You made a commitment to a life spent on taking care of your children, at the expense of your own freedom.

DAVE

You should be damned proud of that, Mrs. Rosato.

FILOMENA

I believe in God.

NEVA

I know you do. And it's not up to us to judge your actions. Just like you should not be judging Carmela. Leave it in his hands. And leave it in Carmela's hands.

DAVE

Oh yeah. My bet is on Carmela. I would bet all my life's belongings that she will do the right thing by this family.

FILOMENA

My son has been through too much. More than anyone should have to bear. He needs to be understood.

NEVA

In many ways, I think Carmela knows him better than you
do.

FILOMENA

I raised him.

NEVA

You may have raised him, but he spilt blood in that desert.
And gone with his spilt blood went a lot of who he was.
Somewhere in the sands of Egypt lies the Silvio you knew.
The Silvio that came after, well, that's where Carmela
comes in. And that's the Silvio we have today.

DAVE

You have to let him go, Filomena. He's Carmela's now. And
they need each other. God has a huge memory, and he will
not forget what you did.

FILOMENA takes it all in, as CARMELA enters the kitchen
carrying a blanket. She crosses out into the backyard and places
the blanket on the baby. FILOMENA looks over to CARMELA
with a sign of relief. FILOMENA quietly exits.

DAVE

Georgette and I would love to have you over for dinner
some time. The both of you. It's been a long day, I'll get
out of your way. Good night. Uh ... good night, Carmela.
(*exits*)

CARMELA

Good night, Dave.

NEVA

Carmela. If you need anything ... well ... my window is
right there.

CARMELA

Buona notte, Neva.

NEVA exits. CARMELA looks over to the baby, and then steps back into the house. SILVIO enters the backyard carrying a white calla lily.

SILVIO

What's the matter? They left you all alone. Ah, don't be scared, your father is here. What am I doing talking to a child? Look at you, Luciano, you're barely born and here you are trying to talk to me. What are we going to do with these women, ah, what? You know I would never hurt you. Never. What am I supposed to do? Ah, Luciano, give me the answer. Minsicha! You burped all over yourself. You're going to make me proud. You're going to carry my name, the family name. For me, for your mother, your sisters, for all of us. You'll show them. Won't you? I'm scared, Luciano, I'm scared. I'm going to need you. Understand? I'm going to need you. I'm your father. This is your mother's favourite flower. It's a calla lily. She had a dozen of these on her wedding day. Now if you see me in trouble, just start crying, you know, to get your mother's attention.

CARMELA steps out onto the porch with a sweater over her shoulders. She crosses over to the swing and sits. SILVIO crosses over to the work area. He removes the tarp. He reveals the table. The table is finished. It's a solid piece of work. He moves it to the centre of the yard. He places the calla lily on the table. CARMELA examines the table. She can't help but feel awed by the craftsmanship of the table.

SILVIO

I hope you like it. It's strong. It will last. Did you eat? I'm sure you did. (*pause*) I like your dress. (*pause*) I thought maybe we can go for an ice cream. I know you like it.

CARMELA

I'm not in the mood for ice cream.

SILVIO

In Belgium you never refused ice cream.

CARMELA
That was Belgium.

SILVIO
It was. (*pause*) ... The girls?

CARMELA
They're sleeping.

SILVIO
Are you okay? The breathing, I mean. (*pause*) Carmela, I need you to say something.

CARMELA
I said what I had to say.

SILVIO
I always said the most important thing is respect. And it's something I never gave you. I assumed things ... because of what I went through ... the war ... I felt I was owed things. You should've seen me before the war ... Carmela ... I never told you about the battle for Halfaya Pass. When I pulled the trigger ... when I killed those innocent men ... my life ... I asked you to marry me, and you said yes. Because that's the way we were brought up. But you never knew what you were getting into. This morning, when you let it out ... I swear, Carmela, I swear to God, that I went somewhere in my head, I was ready to attack. I don't know what it was that stopped me. It was your tears. Your tears. My God, I'm hurting, I'm destroying the one I love. Why? Why am I doing that? I don't know. I can't give you an answer. I may have survived Halfaya Pass, but every night I live with the thoughts. That's why I work so hard, so I can fall asleep, so I don't have to think. That maybe I don't have to dream. That maybe I don't have to see those things again. But I can still see them. They never went away. My responsibility with you was to respect you enough to tell you about who I was and where I came from. I didn't do that.

CARMELA

I knew. I knew it all. You never had to tell me.

SILVIO

How did you know?

CARMELA

Your mother. Right after I accepted your marriage proposal. She came to see me … to tell me about your behaviour. Your change in personality. And I also knew about that woman you had in England. And I knew how your mother kept those love letters away from you. And I knew how it broke your heart. I knew it all. I knew it all. She came to protect me from you. And I told her not to worry. That I would take care of her son.

SILVIO

You knew all that? But—How can she defy me like that … that lying old …

CARMELA

See? See how you lose it? Why do you have to get angry? We're having a discussion. How do you know she wasn't testing me? To see if I would accept her son in light of all this information.

SILVIO

It had to be more than that. Accepting me … I mean … there had to be more than just feeling sorry for me.

CARMELA

I didn't feel sorry for you. I admired you. For surviving all that. Pity? Who needs that? You say that all the time.

SILVIO

I do … and I believe that.

CARMELA

Well so do I! When we married, I knew more about you than you knew about me. I had the advantage there. Not you.

SILVIO
There had to be something else?

CARMELA
Of course there was something else! For God's sake ... of all the men in the village that I could've married, and don't think for a moment you were the only one who wanted me.

SILVIO
I wasn't?

CARMELA
I had my choices. I chose you.

SILVIO
Why? With all the information you had? Why?

CARMELA
I was drawn to you. You were mysterious ... and I found that fascinating. You had the looks. I found you handsome.

SILVIO
You did?

CARMELA
Boy, are you thick. Yes, I found you handsome. I got excited by you. And look at me. I'm no pushover.

SILVIO
No, God no.

CARMELA
Do you know how handsome our children are going to be? Look at Maria. A boy is going to snatch her up in no time. Liliana is just shining in white light. And our little boy. You'll see ... just you wait.

SILVIO
I don't know what to make of this.

CARMELA

That's life. Isn't it? There is more to life than just work and
duty. There's passion and love and understanding. And
there are things we just can't put into words.

SILVIO

So. You knew?

CARMELA

I knew everything.

SILVIO

I don't want to lose you. I never want you to leave me
again. Never. I don't know what I'd do without you. (*pause*)
I don't know what's going to come of me. (*pause*) I need to
put the past behind me.

CARMELA

And?

SILVIO

And ... And? Well ... this could take some time.

CARMELA

You have to trust me. With no trust, we have nothing.

SILVIO

I trust you.

CARMELA

If you're not willing to help yourself, then I can't help you.
Understand?

SILVIO

Yes. Well there's nothing more to be said. We have an
understanding?

CARMELA

I don't know.

SILVIO

What are you saying? Come on, don't play with me.

CARMELA
Look at me. Touch me. Touch me like you've never
touched me before. Touch me. (*SILVIO takes her hand.*) Like
you mean it. (*SILVIO kisses her hand.*) Look at me. Not my
breasts. My eyes.

SILVIO
Oh. Carmela, I don't know what to say. You'll never leave
me?

CARMELA
Never.

SILVIO
You promise?

CARMELA
I promise I will never leave you. The only thing that can
separate us is death. I promise you that. Here and now.
Across this table. I promise you that I will never leave you.

SILVIO
Thank you. (*pause*) Carmela. (*pause*) I'm sorry. I'm sorry.
I'm so so sorry.

*CARMELA crosses to the swing and sits. SILVIO stands there
slightly bedazzled. CARMELA begins to weep. SILVIO walks over
to her and sits next to her. He lets her cry for a moment. He
eventually caresses her. She now cries in his arms. He lifts her
chin up and kisses her. They now kiss passionately. Once again,
their passion for each other overwhelms them. They kiss and kiss
like they've never kissed before, as the lights fade slowly to black.*

Scene Three

The next morning. The table is front and centre. DAVE and
NEVA are in the kitchen waiting. DAVE is in civilian clothes.
FILOMENA enters carrying her suitcase.

DAVE

Let me get that for you, Mrs. Rosato. (*He takes the suitcase.*)
I'll put this in the car.

FILOMENA crosses into the backyard, DAVE and NEVA follow
behind her.

FILOMENA

(*about the table*) Che bel lavoro.

NEVA

I don't know what to say.

FILOMENA

Life goes on. Both of you. Watch over those kids. Don't
think bad of me. Those were tough times we lived through.
We made decisions out of desperation. Mistakes were made
by the head. But the heart makes no mistakes.

SILVIO enters carrying a basket of fruit.

SILVIO

Neva. Take this fruit and bring it inside. Dave, go inside
and help Carmela.

NEVA takes the basket and exits. DAVE leaves the suitcase and
exits.

SILVIO

You packed everything?

FILOMENA

All I had was a few dresses and a couple of aprons. What
was there to pack?

SILVIO

You should see how nice the Autumn is here, Ma. All the colours. Beautiful.

FILOMENA

I'm not going to see it.

SILVIO

You know ... all your grandchildren will be coming here. My sister's children, one by one, they'll eventually all be here. You'll have no one there.

FILOMENA

I'll have my friends.

SILVIO

You won't have family.

FILOMENA

I've survived worse.

SILVIO

Do you remember why I became a carpenter? (*pause*) Every time you had to reach up to grab something high, you would stand up on that old decaying chair ... I was a little boy ... and I always thought one day you were going to fall.

FILOMENA

I did. I did fall one day.

SILVIO

I remember, you sprained your ankle. And it frustrated me that I couldn't fix it for you. I kept thinking, where's Pa? Where's my father so he can fix this?

FILOMENA

You were a little boy.

SILVIO

I knew one day I was going to build you a small stepladder. Just three steps so you can reach higher places in the kitchen.

FILOMENA

You built it … you had just turned fourteen years old.

SILVIO

That's right. I built it because I did not want my mother to fall down anymore. I built it so it could last. It was built to help you.

FILOMENA

I remember.

SILVIO

That's why I became a carpenter. I did not want you to fall down anymore. I built that stepladder … and … (*SILVIO is holding back tears.*) I put everything in my soul into that stepladder.

FILOMENA

That was a long time ago.

SILVIO

It was.

FILOMENA

There's nothing more to be said. I never wanted to hurt you. Never. I was scared. Silvio. Figlio mio. Remember one thing: we were the poorest family in the village. No husband … no money … nothing … everyone back home knew we were the poorest. But in my heart I knew I was the richest woman there. Because I had you. I had you. You gave me a reason to live. You saved me. Now I have to let you go, because there comes a time when a mother is of no more use to her child. It's like the little birds who have to leave the nest. Sometimes it's the mother who has to fly away. It has to be done. I can't change the past. But … you have the whole future in front of you. I have very little time left. And I'm not going to use it to be in your way. Now call your family out here.

SILVIO

Carmela!

CARMELA enters the backyard holding the child. DAVE and NEVA follow her out.

SILVIO

(*He takes the baby in his arms. He holds him up towards the sky, admiring him like a shining light. He then gently hands the baby over to FILOMENA. He takes the suitcase and puts it back in the kitchen. He comes back out into the yard.*) Carmela, it's time to eat. Dave, give me a hand with the table. (*pause*) What are you all standing around for? I want my lunch!

FILOMENA places the child in the carriage as she breathes a sigh of relief.

CARMELA

Wait. Leave the table outside. We'll eat out here al fresco. Silvio, help me with the food.

SILVIO

Let's have some wine first.

SILVIO enters the kitchen. CARMELA follows him in. DAVE is examining the table. Eventually he looks underneath it. He sees something that startles him.

DAVE

Neva, did you see this?

NEVA

What?

DAVE

Underneath the table. Silvio wrote something. He etched something into the wood.

NEVA looks. She too seems a little galvanized by what she sees.

DAVE

What does it mean?

NEVA

I don't know.

SILVIO re-enters with a bottle of wine.

119

FILOMENA
Why don't you put on a different shirt?

SILVIO
What's wrong with this one?

FILOMENA
It's Saturday. Put on a Saturday shirt.

SILVIO
Don't start, Ma.

> *CARMELA enters carrying the glasses.*

CARMELA
He looks fine in that shirt.

SILVIO
Mannaggia la miseria! I forgot something. (*SILVIO runs to the work station and reveals a cutting board.*) Neva, I made this for you. You cut your bread on it, your meats, whatever you want.

NEVA
Thank you, Silvio. I feel like I'm part of your family now.

SILVIO
You are, Neva, you are.

SILVIO
Aspetta! Ci vuole la musica!

> *SILVIO runs back inside turns on the phonograph and comes back out. We hear Puccini's "Nessun Dorma" from Turandot playing.*

NEVA
Che bella famiglia!

SILVIO
And it's gonna get bigger. The family will double in no time. I'm going to call over all my nephews. Wouldn't you like that, Ma?

FILOMENA
I miss them so much.

SILVIO
Benito, Romano, Adriano …

FILOMENA
Don't forget Felice.

SILVIO
I'll place my bet on Adriano. My nephew is going to make it big here. With my help, Adriano will be building houses all over this city.

FILOMENA
He's a good boy.

SILVIO
Wait a minute. Ma, Filomena, my niece. (*to DAVE*) I should introduce her to what's his name … you know … your mother's sister's son.

DAVE
You mean my cousin.

FILOMENA
That's what he means.

DAVE
Why don't you just say my cousin?

SILVIO
I don't really know him.

DAVE
He's still my cousin.

SILVIO
Yes … the son of your mother's sister.

DAVE
Which is my cousin.

FILOMENA

Oh Madonna ... Dave, you sure you're not Calabrese?

DAVE

His name is Gioacchino.

SILVIO

That's right Gioacchino. Is he with someone?

DAVE

No.

SILVIO

He should meet my niece. Filomena. Oh, she's a beautiful girl. They'll be great together.

CARMELA

What are you, a matchmaker now?

SILVIO

I think Gioacchino and Filomena will make a great couple. Don't you think?

DAVE

It won't hurt to try.

SILVIO

I'll get her over here.

DAVE

So, Silvio, you gonna tell me what that means?

SILVIO

Listen to the music. "Nessun Dorma." This is a song about a man who never loses hope. I will teach you the whole opera one day.

CARMELA

(*crosses to the side of the house*) Maria! Liliana! Vieni! Vieni! E tempo di mangiare!

DAVE

What you wrote underneath the table. What does it mean?

SILVIO
One day, my little boy will explain it to you.

CARMELA
Buona salute a tutti!

EVERYONE
Salute!

THE END.